Romans

DAILY BIBLE COMMENTARY

A Guide for Reflection and Prayer

Romans

James D. G. Dunn

HENDRICKSON
PUBLISHERS

Romans
Daily Bible Commentary
Hendrickson Publishers, Inc.
P. O. Box 3473
Peabody, Massachusetts 01961-3473

ISBN 978-1-59856-190-6

Printed in the United States of America

First Printing — April 2007

Library of Congress Cataloging-in-Publication Data

Dunn, James D. G., 1939–
    Romans / James D.G. Dunn.
        p. cm. — (Daily Bible commentary ; 6)
    ISBN 978-1-59856-190-6 (alk. paper)
    1. Bible. N.T. Romans—Commentaries. 2. Bible. N.T. Romans—Devotional literature. I. Title.
    BS2665.53.D86 2007
    227'.107—dc22
                                                    2007003370

Introducing the
Daily Bible Commentary
Series

A Guide for Reflection and Prayer

Congratulations! You are embarking on a voyage of discovery—or re-discovery. You may feel you know the Bible very well; you may never have turned its pages before. You may be looking for a fresh way of approaching daily Bible study; you may be searching for useful insights to share in a study group or from a pulpit.

The Daily Bible Commentary series is designed for all those who want to study the Scriptures in a way that will warm the heart as well as instruct the mind.

• If you have never really studied the Bible before, the series offers a serious yet accessible way in.

• If you want to have both head and heart knowledge of the Bible, the series helps you first understand what the Bible is saying and then reflect on its meaning in your life and in the way you pray.

• If you help to lead a church study group, or are otherwise involved in regular preaching and teaching, you can find invaluable "snap-shots" of a Bible passage through the Daily Bible Commentary approach.

• If you are a church worker or pastor, looking to recharge your faith, this series could help you recover the wonder of Scripture.

To help you, the series distills the best of scholarly insights into straight-forward language and devotional emphasis. Explanation of background material and discussion of the original Greek and Hebrew will always aim to be brief.

Using a Daily Bible Commentary

The series is designed for use alongside any version of the Bible. You may have your own favorite translation, but you might like to consider trying a different one in order to gain fresh perspectives on familiar passages.

Many Bible translations come in a range of editions, including study and reference editions that have concordances, various kinds of special indexes, maps, and marginal notes. These can all prove helpful in studying the relevant passage.

The Daily Bible Commentaries are designed to be used on a daily basis, with you reading a short passage from the Bible and then learning more about it from the commentary entry. Alternatively, it can be read straight through, or it can be used as a resource book for insight into particular verses of the biblical book.

While it is important to deepen our understanding of a given passage, this series always aims to engage both heart and mind in the study of the Bible. The Scriptures point to our Lord himself and our task is to use them to build our relationship with him. When we read, let us do so prayerfully, slowly, reverently, expecting God to speak to our very being.

Contents

IV The process incomplete: sin, law, flesh, death

V The process incomplete: Israel

ROMANS: INTRODUCTION

Paul's letter to the Christians in Rome is probably the single most important letter ever written by a Christian. As an explanation of the Christian faith, it is arguably the most important Christian document of all time. It has played a crucial role in forming and shaping the faith of the first Christians, no doubt from the day it was first read out in the Roman churches. It became the core round which the other Pauline letters were collected, to become a fundamental part of the emerging New Testament. As the most comprehensive theological statement within the New Testament canon, it became the basis for creeds and confessions down through the centuries. It has formed the deep foundations of Christian theology, its full significance often hidden from generations who have affirmed teachings of whose authorization in Paul's writing they were unaware. Even those who have reacted against the over-dogmatization of the Christian faith have found that they could not ignore Romans. And any attempt to reformulate what Christians believe has had to interact with Romans. Most of the greatest minds within Christian history have acknowledged their debt to Romans. And countless individuals, including Augustine, Luther and Wesley, have traced their entry into faith to words from Romans.

To be able to spend time with Paul's letter to the Romans is a privilege to be cherished. To interact seriously with the thought of Romans is to undertake a profoundly intellectual and perspective-transforming journey. To enter deeply into the spirit of Romans is to open oneself to a faith-enriching and life-motivating experience. May you find it to be so.

Paul the missionary

Paul wrote his letter to the Christians in Rome some time in the mid- to late-50s of the first century. We don't know when he was born, but he himself was probably in his mid-50s when he wrote.

After his conversion in the early 30s, and an adjustment period, he had worked as a teacher and preacher for about fifteen years, first in his native Cilicia (south-east corner of modern Turkey) (Galatians 1:21), and then in the church at Antioch (Syria) (Acts 13:1), and then as its missionary (the first missionary journey) (Acts 13—14). The last six years or so he had devoted to missionary work round the

Aegean, principally in Corinth (Greece) and Ephesus (across the Aegean) (Acts 16—19). But now he believed he had done what needed to be done in that region. Churches had been well established, and missionaries were going out from them into towns and cities further from the coast—like Epaphras of Colossae. It was time to look to new mission fields.

Perhaps because he was pursuing a grander design, of which we now have only hints, he saw the next and probably climactic goal of his work in Spain—completing a half-circle of the northern Mediterranean. But to get to Spain he could hardly bypass Rome. Rome was the capital city of the greatest empire Europe has ever seen, and he would need the support of the Christians there if he was to press further west into a territory (Spain) where, so far as we can tell, there were few Jewish communities. And so he began to compose and dictate to Tertius (Romans 16:22) his most ambitious and comprehensive letter—probably from Corinth during the three months mentioned in Acts 20:3.

There was an initial embarrassment to be dealt with. Paul had made a firm resolve only to undertake pioneer missionary work. He did not want to interfere with other missions and their way of doing things. He did not want to 'build on another man's foundation' (Romans 15:20). He was even more fierce in his insistence that no other missionaries should interfere with his work. He had had quite enough experience of that with his churches in Galatia (Galatians) and Corinth (2 Corinthians 10—13), and he had no hesitation in setting out his principles on the point (2 Corinthians 10:13–16).

But there were already churches in Rome. So although Paul as 'apostle to the Gentiles' (Romans 11:13) had some claim on the attention of these churches, he had also to be true to his principles. Hence the slightly hesitant self-introduction in 1:11–15, and the delay in asking for help till 15:22–24, 28–29. The main task of the letter, however, was to fill out the rationale (theology) which underpinned his whole work. At the end of what was probably the most successful and most significant decade of Christian mission of all time (in consequences if not in numbers), it was fitting that Paul should pause, review his gospel message and set it out with due care for his potential supporters.

Rome, the church at the centre

Who founded the Roman churches, we do not know. Tradition says that it was Peter and Paul. But we know that is not the case with Paul. He writes to Christians already there, to prepare for his first visit. Perhaps it was Andronicus and Junia, the only named apostles whom the New Testament actually locates in Rome (Romans 16:7). Or possibly churches emerged from within the various Jewish synagogues as the stories about Jesus' death and resurrection began to circulate within and among the synagogues through traders and visitors.

We know that there were many Jews in Rome. There are various references to their numbers stretching back more than a hundred years before Paul's letter. One informed guess puts the number at 40,000 to 50,000, mostly living, it would appear, in Trastevere (across the Tiber). We should also remember that the earliest movement which became known as Christianity began as a renewal movement within the Judaism of the time. A new development would begin, with individuals who had come to believe that Jesus was Messiah speaking about their new belief to fellow Jews, or with a visiting speaker speaking about Jesus in public. Acts tells us that Paul always began his mission in a new place at the local synagogue. One of the main reasons would have been that there was usually a fairly large number of Gentiles attracted by Judaism (in particular by its austere monotheism, its practice of observing one day in seven for rest, and its high sexual ethic). They are usually called 'God-fearers'. They would have often attended gatherings at the local synagogue, and as they were already sympathizers with Judaism, they would be fertile ground for the seed gospel of a Jewish Messiah for Gentiles.

Something like this must have happened within the synagogues of Rome. As interest spread, there would have been gatherings on the subject, in the synagogue itself, or, more likely, in the homes of believers and sympathizers. We hear of several 'churches in the home' in Paul's letters. Priscilla and Aquila seem to have been particularly active in this respect (Romans 16:3; 1 Corinthians 16:19).

In many places this must have happened quite peaceably, with 'home churches' functioning as house groups attached to one or more synagogues. But in Paul's experience tensions often grew between synagogue and home church and resulted in a breach. Paul was writing from a church which had known this painful experience (Acts 18:1–11). And a slightly obscure reference in the Roman historian

Suetonius indicates something similar in Rome. He tells us that the Emperor Claudius 'expelled Jews from Rome because of their constant disturbances at the instigation of Chrestus' (*The Twelve Caesars: Claudius* 25.4). Suetonius' information was probably somewhat muddled: he thought 'Christ' (Christus would sound like Chrestus) was active in the troubles. The more likely cause is that the message about Jesus as Messiah (the equivalent to 'Christ' in Greek) was causing the sort of upset and hostility that we read of in Acts (13:45; 14:19; 17:5; 18:12–13; 19:9). The emperor got fed up with the resulting disturbances and expelled those regarded as the troublemakers. Among them were Aquila and Priscilla. One good result was that the expulsion made possible their meeting Paul in Corinth (Acts 18:2), resulting in one of the most fruitful partnerships in Christian history (Romans 16:3–4).

The expulsion probably took place in AD49, only about six years before Paul's letter was written. That may well have had serious consequences for the embryonic Christian churches. For if Priscilla and Aquila are at all typical, the initial leadership of the house-group churches must have been largely, if not exclusively, Jewish. And if these Jews were regarded as the troublemakers, then it is quite possible that most of the leaders of the young churches were expelled. In their absence, Gentiles may have had to step into the gap, and the house groups in consequence may have become more estranged from the synagogues which still functioned. But now, with Claudius dead and his decree lapsed, Jews like Aquila and Priscilla could return to Rome, and their return may have caused a further strain within little churches led for the previous five years by Gentiles. Most of this is speculative. But something like this probably lies behind the situation envisaged in Romans 14.

A further cause of concern would be the fact that these home churches were meeting in the capital city itself. The Roman authorities were always very suspicious about groups and societies, lest they be subversive. It was only Julius Caesar's sympathy for the Jewish population in Rome that exempted the synagogues from prohibitive legislation. But now these new little groups were growing, and in an ambivalent relation to the synagogues. How would they be regarded by the authorities? The earlier expulsions of Jews show how drastic measures taken against suspect groups could be. And the emperor's chief officials had no shortage of spies and informers to keep them up to date with what was happening in the back streets. Christians would have to be circumspect. Paul no doubt had this in mind when he wrote Romans 13.

Why Romans?

So the purpose of Romans was probably quite complex.

1. It had a missionary purpose. As apostle to the Gentiles, Paul saw his objective as to bring in 'the full number of the Gentiles', though he also had a view to the impact of that success on his own fellow Jews (Romans 11:13–15, 25–26). He did not see his task as bringing the gospel to Rome, though he looked forward to sharing with them their common faith (1:11–12). His principal missionary goal, however, was Spain. And for that he needed their support, probably financial and in provision of members of his team, and certainly in their prayers (15:22–32).

2. It had an apologetic purpose. Paul wanted to explain his understanding of the gospel, and why he undertook his mission. The principal concern here was to explain two things to what were now largely Gentile congregations: first, why the Jewish heritage (not just the Old Testament) which informed the gospel (the basis of their new life) was so important; and second, why most Jews seemed to be rejecting that gospel. The fact that Paul spends nearly eleven chapters on this theme shows just how important it was to him. The thematic statement given in 1:16–17 indicates that 'the righteousness of God', including the idea of the faithfulness of God, is the principal theme of the whole letter. But the two most prominent sub-themes of the letter could be summed up as 'Jew first and also Greek', and the (Jewish) law, so fundamental to Jewish identity and living.

    In writing this apologia for the gospel, Paul also had half an eye to his immediate next task—to take to Jerusalem the collection made by the Gentile churches for the poor Christians there (15:25–27). For he was all too conscious that his reputation among the more traditionalist Jewish believers was negative. He feared for the outcome of his trip to Jerusalem (15:30–31). So his writing to Rome may also represent the arguments he might have to produce before Jewish Christian gatherings in Jerusalem.

3.   It had a pastoral purpose. Although Paul had never previously visited Rome, his links with people such as Priscilla and Aquila would have given him a fairly clear picture of the strains and challenges confronting the young churches in Rome. In his letters he usually made a point of including a final section of exhortation, directed as much as possible to the particularities of their situation. This seems to be the case with Romans 12:1—15:13.

The structure of the letter

I.   Introduction (1:1–17): greetings (1:1–7); personal explanations (1:8–15); thematic statement (1:16–17).

II. The wrath of God on human unrighteousness (1:18—3:20): on humankind (1:18–32); on Jew first (2:1—3:8); on all without exception (3:9–20).

III. God's saving righteousness to faith (3:21—5:21): to faith in Jesus Christ (3:21–31); Abraham as test case (4:1–25); the new perspective on the future, past and present (5:1–21).

IV. The outworking of the gospel to the individual (6:1—8:39): does grace encourage sin? (6:1–23); what about the law? (7:1–25); tension and fulfilment through the Spirit (8:1–30); the triumph of God (8:31–39).

V.   The outworking of the gospel in relation to Israel (9:1—11:36): what then of Israel? (9:1–5); the call of God (9:6–29); the word of faith (9:30—10:21); the mystery of God's faithfulness (11:1–32); in adoration (11:33–36).

VI. The gospel for every day (12:1—15:13): the basis for responsible living (12:1–2); the body of Christ (12:3–8); love as the norm (12:9–21); living as good citizens (13:1–7); love of neighbour (13:8–10); the imminence of the end (13:11–14); the problem of food laws and holy days (14:1—15:6); conclusion— God's mercy and faithfulness, to Jew first but also Gentiles (15:7–13).

VII. Conclusion (15:14—16:27): Paul's mission and travel plans (15:14–33); final greetings (16:1–23); concluding doxology (16:25–27).

GREETINGS *to a* STRANGE CHURCH

Paul writes to a church which he had not founded and which he had never visited. But where these Christians lived was the capital of the empire, the centre of the Mediterranean world. How, then, should he introduce himself, and how address them?

The writer

Paul calls himself both 'slave' and 'apostle' (v. 1). 'Slave' is a nice blend of humility and dedication. A slave was usually the lowest in any society's pecking order. At the same time, the image was familiar in Jewish worship as an expression of Yahweh's ownership of Israel (e.g. Nehemiah 1:6, 11) and had been used for Moses (e.g. Psalm 105:26) and the prophets (e.g. Jeremiah 7:25). Paul probably had Isaiah 49:1–7 particularly in mind (cf. Galatians 1:15 with Isaiah 49:1–6; Philippians 2:16 with Isaiah 49:4). That is to say, he probably saw himself as carrying forward the Servant of God's mission to be 'a light to the Gentiles'.

The word 'apostle' indicates a messenger sent with the authorization of the sender, to act in his name and to represent him. Paul had had to insist on the title in his own case, because of the unusual circumstances of his commissioning (Galatians 1:1, 11–12). It was crucial to him (and for Christianity) that the authenticity of his commission had been accepted by the Jerusalem leadership (Galatians 2:7–9). For him, an apostle was pre-eminently a missionary and church founder (1 Corinthians 9:1–2; 2 Corinthians 10:13–16). He saw himself as primarily 'apostle to the Gentiles' (Romans 11:13).

So it is Paul's total commitment to 'the gospel of God', the good news from God, which he emphasizes from the first word. The readers, who didn't know Paul personally, could be confident that he was writing out of no factional or sectional interest, and with the full backing of the one who sent him.

The recipients

In particular, Paul stresses that his commission is to the 'nations/ Gentiles' (v. 5), which must include the Roman Christians in some sense (v. 6). This is slightly surprising, since the way in which the gospel came to Rome was probably through Jewish merchants and visitors. In most cases Gentiles first heard the gospel as 'God-fearers', that is, adherents of the local synagogue. The Christian house groups would presumably have begun to operate in some degree of separation from the synagogues. And many Jews had subsequently been expelled from Rome by Emperor Claudius (cf. Acts 18:2), leaving some of the house groups principally or solely Gentile in composition —a factor probably in the situation envisaged in 14:1 to 15:6 (see Study 72). Unusually, however, Paul does not use the term 'church' to describe the Christians in Rome—perhaps because they could only meet in scattered houses (16:5) and not as a single assembly ('church'). (We will return to this in Study 83.)

This opening, then, sets up the dynamic of the letter: it was written by a Jewish apostle to Gentiles; and on the theme of a Jewish gospel about a Jewish Messiah. Paul makes the point with some care even before his greeting is complete. This gospel was promised in the sacred scriptures (v. 2). It is about one who was the seed of David (v. 3). And the readers are greeted in terms which had traditionally designated Israel—'beloved of God, called to be saints' (v. 7). Evidently, a central point for Paul in this letter is that Gentiles were being brought, not least through his own preaching, into a relationship with God previously enjoyed only by Israel. The ramifications of all this are what makes this letter so intriguing, as we shall see.

The greeting itself is a beautiful blend of Greek and Hebrew tradition (v. 7). The Greek word 'grace' (*charis*), very similar to the more typical Greek greeting (*chairein*), sums up the character of God's dealings with his human creatures, as motivated by and expressive of God's generosity from start to finish. And 'peace' (*shalom*) is the traditional Jewish greeting, where the thought is not simply of peace of mind but of general well-being. Paul's wish for these Roman Gentiles is that they should experience the richness of the peace cherished by Israel combined with the grace so fully manifested in Jesus.

PRAYER

We thank you, O God, for Paul who did so much to bring
the gospel to the Gentiles. In reading this account of the gospel
he brought, help us to appreciate the strength of its Jewish
character and the wonder of a grace that reaches out
to the nations as a whole.

The GOSPEL *of* GOD

An early confession of faith

It looks as though Paul has deliberately inserted into his extended greeting an already formulated statement of the gospel. The indications that an earlier formula is being quoted are the confessional form of the statement ('concerning his Son, who…'), and the parallel phrases in the twin lines:

who was descended   from the seed of David   in terms of the flesh

who was appointed   Son of God   in terms of the Spirit of holiness
from the resurrection of the dead.

Various echoes of such statements have been identified in a number of Paul's letters. In Romans itself we will notice 4:24–25; 5:6, 8; 7:4; 8:11, 32, 34; 10:9; another famous fragment is 1 Corinthians 15:3–4.

In including this passage even within his greetings, Paul presumably intended to provide further reassurance to the Roman believers regarding his credentials. If any hints or echoes of the controversies confronting Paul in some of his mission centres (e.g. Galatians) had reached those in Rome, it would be important to reassure them that Paul was not only an acknowledged apostle of God but also that the gospel he preached was what they themselves knew as the gospel. The formula is used again in 2 Timothy 2:8.

It is worth noting that Christianity, from its earliest days, found it necessary to express its gospel and faith in confessional or credal statements. The same need was confirmed in the controversies which marked the early centuries of Christianity, and was fufilled in the familiar Apostles' and Nicene Creeds. Such statements are still necessary and desirable, partly because the faith does need to be expressed in words, partly to serve as badges by which fellow believers can be recognized, and partly as utterances which bond even strangers in common faith and worship, as presumably here.

Confessing Jesus

The confession focuses on the two most important aspects of Christian faith regarding Jesus. He was the royal Messiah, the son of David, expected by Israel. But he was also Son of God. This can be subsequently expressed in more general terms of Jesus' humanity and divinity. But given the point made in Study 1 (1:1–7), not to mention the tragic tradition of Christian anti-semitism, it is important to note that the humanity here confessed is that Jesus was Jesus the Jew.

The confession also puts great weight on the resurrection of Jesus. 'He was appointed ('declared' or 'designated', as in some translations, is too weak) Son of God in power from the resurrection'. This does not mean that Jesus only became Son of God at the resurrection; the whole formula is a confession of God's Son (v. 3). But it does mean that the resurrection marked a distinctive new phase, even a new 'becoming' for Christ. It may even be the case that the phrase 'from the resurrection of the dead' (rather than 'from his resurrection from the dead') echoes an early understanding that Jesus' resurrection was part and/or the beginning of the final resurrection. This would underline still more the epochal character of what the first Christians believed had happened. At any rate, the passage underlines the centrality of the resurrection of Christ for Christian faith, and how, in effect, all deeper insight into the reality and status of Christ flowed from the conviction that God had raised him from the dead.

Paul reinforces this last point by adding at the end of the formula quoted, 'Jesus Christ our Lord' (v. 4), by identifying the Lord Jesus as the medium through whom Paul had received his grace and apostleship (v. 5), and by linking 'the Lord Jesus Christ' with 'God our Father' in the final greeting (v. 7). Central to Christian insight into God is that God has revealed himself through Christ and that God's character as Father has been given clearest definition by the character of Jesus' life, death and resurrection.

PRAYER

We praise you for Jesus, son of David and Son of God,
and above all for the resurrection in which our own hope is rooted.
Help us to grow in our understanding and appreciation
of that faith and to confess it the more fully.

3

THANKSGIVING, HOPES & APOLOGIES

Paul's prayer for the Christians in Rome

Paul follows the convention of the time in adding to his introductory greeting a prayer of thanksgiving for the recipients of the letter (v. 8). He does not ignore such courtesies, and even if the language is exaggeratedly polite ('all over the world') its good intention would no doubt have been appreciated. It is a teaching technique familiar to all teachers, but the importance of words of commendation in Christian communication is still worth noting, since they can provide an often-needed reassurance for individuals and can help to build a proper self-respect in communities. Sadly, however, most Christians seem quicker to criticize one another than to praise.

Given the reflection of 1:3–4 (Study 2), it is worth noting that the prayer is offered to God 'through Jesus Christ' (as also in 7:25). Prayer is only rarely offered to Jesus as such in the New Testament (10:13; 2 Corinthians 12:8). In Paul, the typical prayer terms (as in v. 10) are usually addressed to God and never to Christ, as also a key worship term like 'glorify' (e.g. 1:21; 11:36; 15:6–7, 9).

Equally courteous is Paul's reassurance that he remembered the Roman Christians in his prayers (vv. 9–10). But he protests the point strongly ('God is my witness'), so that we can be sure that Paul did indeed spend much time in prayer. We can well imagine that on his long journeys by foot or by ship he made good use of much of the time to remember before God his churches and the individual members whom he knew, many of whom had been converted through his ministry.

Travel plans

Paul was particularly keen to visit the churches in Rome (v. 10). The principal reason becomes apparent only later (15:23–24), but the recipients would be well aware of how strategic was their position in the capital city of the empire (all roads lead to—and from—Rome). Much of Paul's letter-writing was to arrange visits and to explain why plans had had to be changed (v. 13); compare 2 Corinthians 1:15—2:4. Such notes give us a vivid sense of Paul's breadth of vision and concern, and of how important he believed it to be to maintain communication with and between his churches, both by visiting them personally and by letter as a kind of substitute for his being absent.

Paul's pastoral sensitivity comes out clearly in his statement of intent: 'I long to see you, that I may share with you some spiritual gift so that you may be strengthened' (v. 11). But then, immediately, he catches himself. He did not found their congregations; he is not their apostle (cf. 15:20). The relationship between him and this church, already flourishing before he visited it, was more one of equals, of fellow believers ministering to each other (v. 12).

In the same tone he freely admits his indebtedness to Greeks and barbarians, to wise and foolish (v. 14). In the first half of each pair he in effect acknowledges the benefit of a classical education, not least in terms of his mastery of a language (Greek) which was a vehicle of communication throughout the Mediterranean world, but also in terms of the skills of communication (rhetoric) which he had, no doubt, learned in his education as a youth in Tarsus. At the same time, he indicates a similar indebtedness to those whom the well-educated Greek would have regarded as inferior—the other nationalities (including his own), and the low-born, poorly educated, without power and influence (cf. 1 Corinthians 1:18—2:5).

The emerging impression of Paul is rather more attractive than the much harsher, authoritarian, uncompromising portrait of popular opinion. This Paul has a nice turn of compliment, is a sensitive pastor, and makes humble acknowledgment of his indebtness to lowly regarded as well as highly regarded. The impression is strengthened when such passages as 14:1—15:6 and 1 Corinthians 7 and 9 are read with care and with a sensitivity that matches his writing.

PRAYER

We give you thanks for those who are encouragers, as well as those
who are teachers and counsellors. Grant us the sensitivity in all our
various relationships to know when to praise and when to criticize,
when to admit weakness and fault and when to stand our ground;
and give us words to speak which build up,
and not just words which break down.

The RIGHTEOUSNESS *of* GOD

Nothing to be ashamed of

Paul's introductory words have led up very neatly to the main subject of his letter. This is the summary of the gospel which he preaches and which he wants to share with the Romans. These verses, therefore, form the principal thematic statement of the letter; the main body of the letter that follows will, in effect, be an exposition of this statement.

His opening words ('not ashamed of the gospel') may well echo Jesus' own warning not to be ashamed over Jesus' words (Mark 8:38; Luke 9:26), in which case Paul implies that he understood his gospel to be in direct continuity with Jesus' own teaching. The gospel focused on Jesus' death and resurrection was not to be thought of as superseding or making irrelevant Jesus' own earlier teaching.

The main reason for Paul's confidence, however, is that the gospel is 'the power of God for salvation'. By this Paul means that the preaching of this message actually has the effect of bringing about 'salvation', that is, wholeness (the imagery is of bodily health), preservation and final deliverance. This was something that was borne out by Paul's own experience—the gospel experienced as a convicting, transforming power among those who responded to it (e.g. 1 Corinthians 2:4–5; Galatians 3:2–3; 1 Thessalonians 2:13). Throughout all his writings, Paul seeks to maintain a similar blend between being convinced in mind, convicted in heart and committed in will.

To all who believe

The dynamic character of the gospel is explained by reference to 'the righteousness of God' and by elaboration of 'faith'. The former phrase was the one which had caused Martin Luther such despair prior to his illumination. For he had been taught and thought that it denoted God's judicial righteousness, in accordance with which he punished sinners. But then Luther realized that in the usage of the Old Testament, God's righteousness means God's *saving* righteousness, by which he reckons sinners as righteous (Romans 4:4–5 is a key passage). In fact, the term is often rendered 'deliverance' or 'vindication' in modern translations of the Psalms and Isaiah (e.g. Psalm

51:14; 98:2; Isaiah 51:5–8; 62:2). The point is that 'righteousness' in Hebrew thought refers to the fulfilment of obligation which arises out of relationship. In reference to God, it denotes the fulfilment of the obligation which God had taken upon himself in creation, to sustain it (cf. Genesis 8:22), and in his covenant with Israel, to sustain and 'deliver' them.

The distinctive feature of Paul's understanding of this righteousness is that it was now to be freely offered to *all* who believe, not just Jews but also Greeks. That was the revolutionary nature of the gospel he preached—that the special privileges hitherto enjoyed by Israel as God's people were now open to all who believed. This 'all who believe' becomes a leading motif throughout the central section of the letter (e.g. 3:22; 4:11; 10:4, 11).

The triple mention of 'faith' in verse 17 rams the point home and prepares for the later exposition of chapters 3 and 4. What precisely Paul meant by 'from faith to faith' is unclear—possibly from God's faith(fulness) to be received by (human) faith; or by 'faith' from start to finish. Either way, the importance of faith, and of faith alone on the human side, is clearly indicated as the only means by which God's saving righteousness may be received.

Paul concludes this key statement by indicating its scriptural warrant ('as it is written')—Habakkuk 2:4. The Hebrew original reads, 'The righteous person by his faithfulness shall live.' The Greek version of Habakkuk 2:4 reads, 'The righteous person by my (God's) faithfulness shall live.' Paul quotes the text in a more open way, so that 'by faith' can be understood as referring either to the noun ('the person who is righteous by faith') or to the verb ('shall live by faith'). Either way, the text underscores the importance of 'faith'. Paul will provide an exposition of what 'faith' involves in chapter 4. For the moment we may simply describe 'faith' as trust in God.

PRAYER

It is a mystery to us as creatures and human beings why you have made us and called us, why you have committed yourself to your creation and to human beings in this wholly generous and uncalled-for way. Teach us to be open to your grace, to receive it for our wholeness, and to live by it from day to day.

5   ROMANS 1:18–25

RELIGION GONE WRONG

The root of all evil

To expound his principal theme (1:16–17), Paul turns at once to a denunciation of human failure. The implication is that it is this human failure which is being addressed by the gospel. By that is meant, not that human failure prompted God to a new way of addressing his human creation, but that human failure has underlined the need for the human creature to return to God as God. The parallel between the wording of verse 17 and verse 18 also implies that 'the righteousness of God' and 'the wrath of God' are two sides of the one coin. Those who recognize and trust in God's commitment to his creation and to his people experience God's righteousness. Those who turn their backs on God experience God's wrath. But neither insight can be worked out by human ingenuity; it has to be 'revealed'.

What is God's wrath? This paragraph and the next (1:26–32) make it clear that 'the wrath of God' describes primarily the moral structure of creation and society. Human choice entails certain consequences; we are free to choose, but we are not free to choose the consequences of our choice. Paul's point is that this is not a mechanical effect, but is God-willed. Precisely because we are not robots but human beings, choices can and have to be made, and our choices help to shape our characters and relationships. Choice is, then, never amoral or non-moral; every personal choice is a choice to be a particular kind of person.

The indictment is summarized in verse 18: humans are characterized by 'impiety' (literally lack of worship), 'unrighteousness' (failure in basic obligations), and suppression of 'the truth' (unwillingness to recognize the truth of God as Creator and of human dependence on God). The basic fault is then spelt out, echoing the narrative of Adam and Eve and their 'fall' in Genesis 2—3. Human beings instinctively know that they are creatures of a divinely powerful Creator (vv. 19–20). But, like Adam, they have failed to acknowledge God as God (v. 21); they have fallen before the temptation that they can be independent of God, that they can be wise in their own right (v. 22). Consequently, they have not become 'like God' (Genesis 3:5), but, in contrast, have become less able to function as truly human—'futile in their thinking', 'their foolish hearts darkened' (v. 21). Their predicament is summed up precisely in verse 22: they think they are wise, and fail to recognize their folly. They think they are mature, 'come of age', able to bear complete responsibility for themselves on their own, and forget that they are but dust. These words are deserving of considerable reflection in any Christian group; if Paul's insight is right here, he does indeed provide a key to analysing the symptoms of all human failure.

The clearest expression of this folly is idolatry. Human beings have abandoned the one God and Creator. But instead of becoming God-like (Genesis 3:5), they have simply begun to worship other gods. Instead of being free and independent, they have become dependent on mere things. Human creatures will always be dependent; that is their given nature. For all that they can create and invent, they can never truly be god/God themselves; they can only project the status of god on to others. Paul evidently perceives it to be a fundamental human instinct to invest ultimate significance in something or some person or some cause to live and die for. Instead of the glorious God, they give their devotion to what is, at best, a mere reflection of their own God-given abilities.

Ironically, they have substituted religion for God. The human creature will never escape the instinct to reverence. But when the invisible Creator becomes too (apparently) remote, or too demanding, humankind will try to satisfy this instinct with a more visible or more comfortable deity or idol—the easy fix of cheap religion. The clearest sign of loss of God is made-to-measure religion, religion where humankind is in control, where the desire of some to lord it over others is given scope. The tragedy is that all religion, Christianity not excluded, gives scope to this sort of self-delusion, of human manipulation of others, of traditions and practices which have more of human folly than of divine wisdom in them. God save us from religion!

PRAYER

Lord, we confess that all too often we make our gods in our own image, because we are more comfortable with a god who is like us, a god who affirms us as we are. Open our eyes to see what we already know in our heart of hearts about our Creator and about our creatureliness, and save us from ourselves for yourself.

6   ROMANS 1:26–32

SOCIETY *in* DECAY

Disoriented sexuality

The course of social decay is charted in the thrice repeated, '(Wherefore) God gave them over to' (1:24, 26, 28). This is the wrath of God—that God gives human beings what they have most desired. The moral consequences of choices determined by self-assertion and self-satisfaction are that 'desire' (a quite proper human emotion) becomes 'lust' (the same word, degenerated).

The decay starts in manipulative and corrupting religion (see Study 5). But that first sign of social decay is quickly followed by a second —the decay of sexual relations. In this Paul displays a profound appreciation of these two most powerful psychological and social drives within humankind: one is the impulse to devote ourselves to the greater, to invest some other (thing) with ultimate significance; the other is the impulse to procreate and to seek sexual satisfaction. Both instinctive drives are part of the creation which God pronounced to be good. It is precisely because they are so fundamental to human flourishing and so powerful in determining character and conduct that their corruption is so devastating for humankind.

The fact that Paul thinks at this point particularly of homosexual practice (vv. 26–27) is troublesome for many today. Some try to limit his denunciation to abusive relations (male adults taking advantage of younger boys). But this is not a realistic reading of the text, for lesbian relations are also clearly in view in verse 26, and in verse 27 the inflamed desire is shared by both partners. At the same time, it should be noted that Paul's initial thought is of a variety of 'unclean' and 'dishonouring' sexual practices (v. 24), of which homosexual practice is only one. It may, then, be unjustified to deny that Paul disapproved of homosexual practice; but it is still less justified to ignore his condemnation of a much wider range of sexual practices which he and the biblical tradition clearly regarded as illicit. Above all, it is putting sexuality in place of God, and making sexual satisfaction a substitute for the devotion which God alone deserves, to which Paul objects.

Anti-social behaviour

But the course of social decay reaches its climax not in sexual misde-meanour so much as in the depressing list of social vices in verses 29–31. Idolatry and sexual lust are all-too-easy targets for moralists, and it is all too easy to forget these other vices, in many ways more corrupting in their effect on society. Such 'vice lists', however, were common among teachers of social ethics (see Mark 7:21–22; 1 Corinthians 5:10–11; 6:9–10; Galatians 5:19–21). Here, it should be noted, the list speaks not just of murder and hatred of God, but of 'greed… envy, rivalry, deceit, malice… rumour-mongering, slander, arrogance, boasting'. It is just such a sequence of petty vices, human nastiness and pinpricks on social cohesion which can be so ruinous of community. Paul sees such petty vices as the sign of a disabled mind (v. 28); a mind which does not start from the recognition of God-givenness and of responsibility for others before God will soon find reasons to justify even such behaviour so corrosive of society's interdependence.

Nor will Paul let his readers off the hook (v. 32). They know that such attitudes and behaviour are wrong. And yet they do the same, and they make excuses for others who act in these ways. Here is another feature of the society which Paul has in view—its solidarity in sin, the mutual encouragement among those living in these ways to continue doing so. Paul remains convinced that in the innermost heart of humankind—call it conscience if you will (2:15)—there is a clear enough sense of right and wrong. Even for those who have shut God out of their lives, there is an instinctive recognition that the cosmos is not merely a product of random evolution but is con-structed and functions on the basis of moral values. When Christians can no longer find men and women of goodwill to whom to appeal on moral and ethical issues, then society is indeed in the depths of decay.

PRAYER

Father, we thank you for the fact and power of human sexuality. Show us how to live with it and to channel it appropriately and positively. Teach us to recognize when and how a society is in decay. And help us to live and work for a society where the values and the attitudes which support and build community are cherished and lived out.

7

PRESUMPTUOUS PIETY

Whom is Paul addressing?

Chapters 2—3:8 function as a 'diatribe'; that is, Paul engages in debate with an imagined opponent, like a public speaker arguing with a heckler in the crowd. Who this opponent is has been a matter of dispute. But several features give a clear enough indication.

It is someone who joins with Paul in 'condemning' what the heckler saw also as the low state of religion, sexual practice and human society. So the first clue is the realization that Paul's indictment in 1:18–32 draws heavily on the criticism that Jews living outside Palestine made of what they perceived as typical Gentile religion and morality (cf. Wisdom of Solomon 11—15 in the Apocrypha). It looks as though Paul is imagining one of his fellow Jews applauding Paul's typically Jewish attack on the idolatry and looser sexual morality which would have been more characteristic of the Greeks in particular at that time.

This reading of the opening of chapter 2 is confirmed by Paul's subsequent stress on 'Jew first and also Greek' in 2:9–10, and also by the way in which he slowly strips away the mask which initially hides the identity of the heckler—first by referring to those who are under the law (2:12) or who have the law (2:14), and second by identifying the heckler as a self-designated 'Jew' in 2:17.

What begins to become clear, therefore, is that Paul wants to bring Jew as well as Greek/Gentile under the same indictment before God. The decay in religion and society extends even into the chosen people themselves. Jew as well as Gentile needs to hear the gospel of God's righteousness to faith (1:16–17).

God's people blind to their own sin

In some ways the position of God's own people is even more serious than that of the ungodly, because they assume that they are all right before God, when they are not. By assuming that they can always rely on God's kindness and patience, they actually despise that kindness and patience (v. 4).

In this attack, Paul may well have been thinking of the attitude reflected in Wisdom of Solomon 15:1–2:

But you, our God, are kind and true, patient and in mercy governing all
things. For even if we sin, we are yours, knowing your power; but we will not
sin, knowing that we are reckoned yours.

Note how the affirmation of God's kindness and patience results in just the sort of presumption regarding sin which Paul attacks here. This is a further confirmation of the identity of the dialogue partner in view in verse 1.

There may be another echo of a view that we find quite often in Wisdom of Solomon—that even when the misfortunes striking two different peoples seem very similar, the godly can regard them as discipline, whereas the ungodly should experience them as condemnation. Such a teaching can be a comforting pastoral technique, but it may also obscure the need for repentance.

What Paul has in view, therefore, is that peculiar blindness which often seems to afflict religious people. They see all too clearly the failure of others, and may be quick and vociferous in their condemnation of that failure. But they are astonishingly blind to their own faults, even when they are the same as those they condemn in others. We need only recall the depressing history of sexual immorality and abuse, or financial irregularity, which have brought many a prominent Christian leader to his or her knees—alas, too late! No wonder Jesus warned against trying to pick out the speck in someone else's eye while oblivious to the plank in one's own (Matthew 7:3–5). And it becomes a little clearer why Jesus also taught a prayer which asks for forgiveness for our own sins 'just as we forgive those who sin against us' (Luke 11:4). For as we forgive, so we are forgiven; as we judge others, so will we be judged (Matthew 6:14–15; 7:1–2). The ancient Greek proverb summed it up in two words: 'Know thyself.' And Robert Burns put it in a prayer which we all need to use, 'O would some power the giftie gie us, to see ourselves as others see us.'

PRAYER
Save us, good Lord, from that spiritual blindness which sees
everyone else's sin except our own. Help us to see ourselves as
others see us, and make us quicker to acknowledge our own
failures than to criticize those of others.

The IMPARTIALITY of GOD

Judgment

A characteristic motivation in religion is the fear of God. This can run from a proper reverence and holy awe before the mystery of the divine, to 'fear' in the more common sense of being frightened, even terrified, before the power behind the universe. Acts 5:12–13 provides an example of such holy awe from the earliest days of Christianity. Instinctive to this fear has been the prospect of judgment, of a final reckoning when all wrongs will be righted and when human history and its values will at last be seen in the right perspective.

Basic here too is the confidence that such judgment will be essentially fair. The same (religious?) instinct which informs the school-child of what is fair and what is unfair in the classroom or playground comes to expression in this expectation as well. As children growing up in a mature and settled society tend to assume an innate sense of fairness undergirding that society, so religion tends to assume a fundamental fairness undergirding history as a whole.

Paul both inherits these beliefs and gives them classic expression.

Judgment according to works

God's judgment will be according to the works or deeds which each person has done (v. 6). This is an insight deeply rooted in Jewish and Christian thinking (see, for example, Proverbs 24:12 and Psalm 62:12; and elsewhere in Paul's letters, 2 Corinthians 5:10). The final assessment of a life will take full and fair account of its character and quality—a verdict which will be much more accurate and fair than most media obituaries or assessments by friends or family. Is such belief in final judgment necessary to reinforce a proper sense of responsibility in human beings for their actions? What other sanctions does the responsible society have?

The character of the deeds which will result in a positive verdict, and of those which will result in a negative verdict, is indicated. Worth noting is the fact that Paul spells out that character in broad terms, which all men and women of goodwill would acknowledge. 'Patience in doing what is good', the motivation of wanting to be remembered gratefully by subsequent generations (vv. 7, 10)—that is the sort of life which all would recognize as 'good'.

In contrast, Paul has in mind lives moved by 'selfish ambition', those who do not count truth or doing what is right as important, who deliberately set their hands to what they know is evil (vv. 8, 9)—that is the sort of life which all would recognize as 'not good'. Paul does not attempt to single out particular good deeds or particularly nasty sins. He is characterizing rather than specifying. But we can recall the full range of behaviour listed in 1:22–32.

The character of the judgment is also indicated—on the one hand, 'eternal life', 'glory, honour and peace' (vv. 7, 10); and on the other, 'wrath and anger', 'affliction and distress' (vv. 8, 9). To be noted once again is the use of language which would make sense to women and men of goodwill. The words used are not descriptions of eternal bliss or of hell. Their purpose is rather to stir up in Paul's readers the appropriate motivation for conduct in daily life.

God is fair

The concluding reassurance complements the assurance of verse 6: 'there is no partiality with God' (v. 11). This too is a deeply rooted conviction which Paul inherited from his ancestral religion (see, for example, Deuteronomy 10:17 and 2 Chronicles 19:7). Here it draws the reader back to the underlying theme of this chapter: just because God is the God of Israel, that does not mean that he will be unfairly favourable to Israel. This was a danger which Paul evidently feared his own people were vulnerable to: by assuming that God's choice of Israel ensured a favourable verdict, they were actually hardening their hearts to the repentence which they should have been showing (v. 5). The tension between God's choice of and faithfulness to Israel and his impartiality and even-handedness to all runs through this whole section.

PRAYER

We bow before your judgment, O God. We rejoice that ultimate judgment lies in your hands, and that we can rest in its impartiality. Save us from any self-deception which will dull our conscience and harden our hearts. And strengthen us to be patient in doing good.

9

JUDGMENT *in* ACCORD *with*
GOD'S LAW

In this section, the target of Paul's criticism becomes still clearer. For he introduces talk of 'the law'. And for a Jew like Paul, that could only refer to God's law, the Torah, the law of Moses. This is clear when he talks of 'the nations/Gentiles who do not have the law' (v. 14)—the assumption being that Israel, of course, has the law.

This basic insight, in fact, is the key to a difficult passage. The difficulty is that the gospel speaks of justification (including final acquittal) by faith and not by law, as we shall see later (3:21—5:1), whereas here Paul talks of justification by doing the law (v. 13). How can Paul speak of a final favourable verdict both in terms of faith alone and in terms of deeds done?

The key is to recognize that Paul is still criticizing a presumptuousness which easily follows upon the conviction that God has chosen one group or people and so, by implication, favours them more than others. In this case, the assumption is that the gift of the law to Israel is a mark of God's special concern to show Israel how to live aright. So, being 'in the law' (v. 12), having the law (v. 14), sets Israel apart from the other nations. Paul responds in two ways.

Hearing and doing

First, he points out that everyone who sins will be subject to God's judgment. Sin destroys, whether the sinner is outside the law or inside it (v. 12). This is a point that Paul comes back to on several occasions. It is implicit in the indictment of 1:18–32: 'those who practise such things are worthy of death' (1:32). It is explicit in the assertion that 'the wages of sin is death' (6:23) and in the exposure of sin's role in chapter 7.

To put the same point in other terms, it is not the hearers of the law who are just before God, but the doers of the law shall be justified (v. 13). This should not be seen as an attack on Judaism, since emphasis on doing the law was characteristic of Jewish tradition (e.g. Deuteronomy 4:1, 5–6, 13–14; 30:11–14): the law is not simply to be taught, but to be observed.

What Paul is actually getting at is the assumption on the part of his fellow Jews that there is a necessary link between hearing and doing the law. The Hebrew term for 'hear' has a fuller meaning than the English: it denotes an attentive hearing. In other words, proper hearing results in doing. And since only Israel has the law, and thus only Israel can hear the law, it follows that only Israel can do the law.

The puzzle of the law-doing Gentile

Hence Paul's second point, that in fact there are Gentiles who, despite not having the law, actually do 'by nature' what the law requires. Even though they do not have the law, they are, as it were, 'the law for themselves' (v. 14). They show the effect of the law written in their hearts; their consciences also attest the ethical and moral dilemmas with which they have wrestled (v. 15).

Here is another area of dispute. Did Paul have any specific Gentiles in mind? Was he thinking only of Gentiles who had become Christian? Probably not. He has already spoken in very broad and general terms about the grounds of judgment in 2:7–10. The implication is that Paul was willing to recognize good and evil wherever they manifested themselves. And he did not exclude the possibility that there were Gentiles who, despite lacking instruction in the law, acted in ways and with motivation of which God would approve. Paul here displays an unexpected openness: he was sufficiently sure of the character of his gospel to be confident that such things would become clear in the final judgment, when what was hidden to the eye of the human observer would be revealed (v. 16).

Here, then, is a classic warning not to assume that our clear-cut categories (of those 'in' and those 'out', those acceptable and those unacceptable) necessarily match God's. The effect of God's law may well appear in circles who have never heard God's law. We do well to acknowledge good as such, and to condemn evil as such, even when they appear in the most unexpected groups.

PRAYER

You are the God who sees the reality of human beings and human situations which is hidden from us. Save us from trying to exercise your judgment. Help us to see good and evil wherever they appear, and to applaud the one and to condemn the other.

10   ROMANS 2:17–24

BOASTING & ITS SELF-CONTRADICTION

The benefits of the law

In this passage, Paul gives us a fairly clear picture of the Jewish self-understanding of his day, particularly in relation to other peoples and nations. As one who had been a zealously practising Jew and a Pharisee (Galatians 1:13–14; Philippians 3:4–6), he knew that self-understanding from inside. The attitudes expressed in verses 17–20 were probably the attitudes which he himself had expressed in his pre-Christian past.

'Jew' was not, in fact, a favourite self-designation of Jews (v. 17). 'Jew' (*Ioudaios*) identified too much by reference to territory (Judea, *Ioudaia*); as such, it functioned to distinguish the Jewish people from other peoples, likewise identified by reference to their native territory (Macedonians, Cretans, and so on). The favourite self-designation was rather 'Israel, Israelite', a term which defined by relating to God —God's chosen people. So the choice of 'Jew' here already signifies a self-definition by distinguishing from others.

The confidence of the heckler in being able to call himself a Jew was expressed primarily in his reliance on the law and his boast in God. What Paul recalled of his own time as a practising Pharisee was the assurance that God had chosen his people to be his own and had given them the law to direct them as his people (v. 17). It was by reference to the law/Torah that they were able to recognize and approve 'the things that matter' (v. 18). That was a priceless gift to have—to be able to discern priorities, to distinguish what was really important from secondary issues. Who would not covet that gift?

The sense of privilege which the law gave to Jews had its corollary in their attitude to other nations. They were 'a guide to the blind, a light to those in darkness, an instructor of the foolish…' (vv. 19–20). In other words, the sense of privilege implied both a low estimate of those not so privileged (blind, in darkness, foolish…), and a sense of obligation to those underprivileged (note the echo of such Old Testament passages as Isaiah 42:6–7). We see something similar in modern Western 'civilization' in its disparagement of 'primitive' peoples and a sense of obligation to bring them the light which it enjoys.

The dangers of pious self-deceit

Paul's criticism of his fellow Jew is muted in the first half of this paragraph, not least because he shares his fellow Jew's sense of privilege (3:1–2). But in the second half, his criticism becomes clearer. It begins with his reminder that there are Jews who break the law as blatantly as anyone else (vv. 21–23). And, as the preceding paragraphs clearly indicated (2:1–16), those failures should be regarded in as serious a light as the equivalent sins by non-Jews. In other words, Paul here is not irresponsibly denouncing all Jews as adulterers and temple-robbers. His point is rather that Jews like himself can too easily turn a blind eye to such sins among their own people. They may even defend or excuse some of them, on the same assumption that God will regard such sins lightly because they are committed by members of his chosen people.

We are back, then, with the criticism seen in the first paragraph of this section (2:1–6). This should not be seen as an expression of anti-Judaism, or as an attack on all Jews. Paul, of course, had in mind his own personal history and the particular context in which the earliest churches found themselves, as they emerged within and from the synagogues. But his critique is applicable to all groups who consider themselves specially privileged by God. That sense of privilege can so easily become a sense of superiority, a forgetfulness that the blessing received says nothing about the worthiness or otherwise of those blessed. The problem re-emerges every time a nation or people are given or attain positions of high power within the world community (superpowers): the greater the power, the greater the capacity for self-deceit, the greater the responsibility before God.

PRAYER

How can we truly rejoice in your goodness to us, O Lord, without giving way also to those hateful tendencies either to look down on others or to think that in our case there are always exceptions to the rules? Show us where, by word or deed, we are in danger of causing your name to be dishonoured by others.

11 ROMANS 2:25-29

REAL CIRCUMCISION & GOD'S JEW

Why circumcision is important

Circumcision is a religious ritual which Christians don't much understand or appreciate. Since Christianity's own self-understanding was largely shaped by Paul's letters, Paul's dismissal of the need for circumcision among Gentile believers has given Christianity a generally low view of the act. This is unfortunate.

It is important, then, to realize that circumcision, the cutting of the skin of the male sexual organ, was equivalent to the dedication of the firstborn and of the firstfruits to God. It signified indebtedness to God for life and its fruits. It was an act of commitment of the individual life and of its life-force to God. This was why it provoked the exhortation to circumcise not the flesh but the heart (as in Deuteronomy 10:16 and Jeremiah 4:4): the dedication and commitment must not be superficial, but from deep within. As we shall see later, Paul made a similar point with regard to Christian baptism (6:3–4): a baptism (in water) which was not also a baptism into Christ simply served to devalue the sacrament.

At the same time, circumcision was far from being an act of merely individual piety. From early days in the religion of Israel it became a mark of Israel, of belongingness to the people of God. Anyone who doubts its significance should read Genesis 17:9–14 with care. This presumably is why Paul could actually divide the world into 'circumcision' and 'uncircumcision' (Galatians 2:7–9); the circumcised male organ could stand for the Jewish people as a whole; and the absence of circumcision could stand for all the rest! Christians could do the same with baptism: the world is divided between baptism (those baptized) and unbaptism (those unbaptized).

This is why Paul could reaffirm the importance of circumcision: 'circumcision is of benefit' (v. 25; 3:1–2). It was of value, so long as its significance was rightly appreciated. As a sign of dedication, it counted for nothing if the circumcised person did not live a dedicated life (v. 25). Again, most Christians would want to say the same with regard to baptism: a baptism which does not result in a living of the dedicated life counts for nothing.

Reality and ritual

The other side of the same point is the one already made in 2:14–15. That is, there are those who have never been circumcised, and yet who live the kind of life which circumcision was intended both to symbolize and to stimulate (v. 26). Those who recognize the symbolical character of circumcision should also acknowledge, therefore, that such uncircumcised dedication is what circumcision is really all about, and can therefore be counted as the reality of circumcision. And the corollary is the same: those who display the reality of circumcision will prove to be more accepted by and acceptable to God than those of circumcised flesh but uncircumcised heart (vv. 27–29).

Here again the truth is timeless. Religion can so easily become a series of formal acts, a matter of visible status, outward and superficial. What God looks to is the heart, both the heart of the individual and the heart of the religion. For the Christian, whatever the sacramental theology assumed, it must surely be a matter of common consent that baptism, whenever performed or with however much water, is of little worth if the heart is not baptized and the baptismal life is not lived from the heart. To say 'I am baptized', as though the possibility of saying that was sufficient of itself, is to deny or ignore the very meaning and symbolism of baptism.

When reality and ritual begin to fall apart, then the religion sustained by that ritual is in trouble. The lesson which Jesus taught regarding what really constitutes purity and cleanness (Mark 7:17–23) needs to be learned ever afresh. It was the same lesson that launched the Christian mission beyond Jews to include Gentiles (Acts 10:9–16, 28, 34–35), and it remained at the heart of the gospel for Paul.

PRAYER

Teach me, good Lord, to love you with my heart as well as my body, to love from the heart and not simply in visible act, to seek for your secret praise more than the praise of my fellows, to live the reality of what I am before you and not to be overly dependent on human affirmation.

12 ROMANS 3:1–8

WHAT *of* GOD'S FAITHFULNESS?

Paul's argument in trouble

The logic of Paul's argument to this point has been clear. Humankind as a whole has turned its back on God; thinking itself too wise to need God, it has actually proved its folly, through its idolatry, its disoriented sexuality and its fractured social relations (1:18–32). However, the indictment of these verses was very much from the perspective of Jews as they looked disapprovingly at Gentile ways of life. And there was a real danger that Paul's own people would think they were somehow exempt from the condemnation of 1:32. So the chief line of Paul's argument has been to ensure that his own people recognized their own plight (2:1–11). Even though they were God's chosen people and had the law, that did not mean that God overlooked their sins (2:12–24); circumcision, for all that it was an obligation laid by God on his people, did not of itself guarantee their future vindication (2:25–29).

The more effective this argument was, the more puzzling it would become for many who first heard Paul's letter read. For the obvious conclusion to draw from it was that being a Jew was no advantage, and receiving circumcision was of no value (v. 1). But for Paul, it was equally important to affirm that Jews were indeed God's chosen people as their circumcision attested ('Jew first, but also Greek'). This is where Paul's argument comes into difficulty: Paul wanted to affirm both the universality of human falling short of God, but also God's overarching plan for humankind with Israel as its bridgehead (v. 2). But to affirm both seemed to result in some contradiction. His argument begins to struggle because he cannot avoid raising the issue at this point, but he is not yet ready to tackle it. He needs first to pursue the logic of his universal indictment (3:9–20) and his answer to it (3:21—8:39), before he can return to the questions raised here (chs. 9—11).

The issue is not Jews, but God

The matter is important for Paul, because behind it lies the profoundest of theological issues—the issue of God's faithfulness.

Israel's failure surely calls into question the God who chose and committed himself to Israel: their unfaithfulness proves the ineffectiveness of that choice and commitment, does it not? (v. 3).

The centrality of the issue is hidden in Paul's Greek (and English translations). For it is referred to not only with the actual term 'faithfulness' (v. 3). The same fundamental Hebrew idea of God's constancy and reliability, his faithfulness to those to whom he has committed himself, also underlies the talk of God's 'truth' (v. 4) and God's 'righteousness' (v. 5). The issue is not just the election (of Israel) but whether God is reliable.

The problem, then, is how God can be reliable in two senses—both faithful to those he has chosen, and impartial judge of the world and of sin. The problem is made all the more poignant since human unfaithfulness actually highlights the faithfulness of God more sharply. If the display of God's faithfulness is actually enhanced by the depth of human unfaithfulness, then where does that leave us? Paul can put the dilemma more sharply still: 'If the truth of God has by my lie overflowed to his glory, why am I still judged as a sinner?' (v. 7).

Here we need to note that Paul identifies just the same problem with his own gospel: if human sin enhances the glory of God's grace in still accepting the sinner, then sin is surely a good thing (v. 8). Here again, Paul has been led by the flow of his argument to announce a problem which he is no position yet to answer; he will return to it in 6:1. The point for us to note, however, is that the good news of a gracious God starts not with Christ, but with God's choice of Israel to be his people, or indeed with God's creation of a world which he will also have to judge. But that same good news poses the most fundamental problems of theology: how to affirm a gracious God in face of human evil; how to affirm a divine faithfulness which is not merely an arbitrary favouritism.

PRAYER

*O God, the depth of the mystery of your grace towards
your creation and towards human beings is far beyond our
comprehension; and yet with Paul we find ourselves unable
to do other than to affirm it and to rejoice in it.
May we never take it for granted!*

The INDICTMENT CONCLUDED

All alike under sin

The most common rendering of verse 9 is, 'What then? Are we (Jews) any better off? No, not at all. For we have already charged that all, both Jews and Greeks, are under the power of sin.' That fits well enough as the conclusion to 2:1—3:8, and with what follows, as we shall see. But there is an interesting variation possible: 'What then do we plead in our defence? For we have now charged...'. Either way, the verse marks the conclusion to Paul's indictment. And the outcome is more or less the same: Jews are no better off so far as divine judgment is concerned; even God's choice of Israel does not amount to an adequate defence against the charges mounted.

It is not always appreciated that this is the first mention of one of Paul's key terms in Romans—'sin'. The whole of the previous indictment (1:18—3:8) is so readily described in terms of human (acts of) 'sin'. But Paul evidently wanted to hold back the term itself in order to use it in a more weighty manner. The point is that in Romans, 'sin' most often denotes a superhuman power rather than a human act. 'Under sin' is the language appropriate for a state of subserviency ('under') to an overmastering power (in this case, 'sin'). Since this is Paul's summary of the charges already laid, it thus becomes clear that behind the human failures and abuses already documented lies a power which, in some sense, rules over or determines human conduct. He does not say whether this is a personal power (like Satan, or 'the god of this world', 2 Corinthians 4:4), or simply a way of characterizing the common human experience of being drawn into conduct which one knows to be wrong. But he will have more to say on the subject later (7:7–25). The point is that the gospel will prove itself only by providing an answer to not simply sin the act, but sin the power.

The law confirms it

As often, Paul attempts to underpin a key claim by a scriptural text—obviously because, as a Jew himself, he recognizes the voice of God speaking through these texts. In this case he cites a sequence of texts, perhaps a collection already to hand from previous study of the scriptures. Of the seven citations, five are from the Psalms (14:2–3; 5:10; 139:4; 10:7; 35:2). Normally these Psalms texts would be heard in the synagogue as bolstering the assumption that the (Jewish) righteous could plead against the (Gentile) wicked. But that is the very presumption of Jewish privilege which Paul has been seeking to undermine. And if they are read without that assumption, and linked with the two other texts (Ecclesiastes 7:20 and Isaiah 59:7–8), they actually reinforce the verdict of Romans 3:9: *no* defence remains; *all* are under the same indictment. 'No one' means what it says—'no one is righteous, *not even one*' (v. 10).

We should note the thrust of this climax to Paul's indictment. It is particularly directed at his own people. He makes this plain in verse 19: 'whatever the law says, it says to those within the law'. This is important, since the usual assumption is that verses 19–20 are a universal indictment, directed at everyone even-handedly. That is not quite correct: Paul directs his final charge particularly against his own people, precisely because they have typically understood themselves to be different from the nations and in a favoured situation before God.

This helps us to understand verse 20. For on the normal assumption (an even-handed indictment), it would naturally follow that the 'works of the law' in view are the sort of deeds which everyone might do—characteristically 'good works' by which God's favour might be earned. But when we see that Paul is particularly targeting his own people, the more obvious meaning is that the 'works of the law' are what Jews in particular do. In other words, Paul in this summary phrase seems to have the same attitude in view that he criticized in 2:17–29 and turned on its head in 3:9–19. 'Works of the law' indicate that kind of obedience to the law which the typical Jew of Paul's acquaintance assumed demonstrated his place within the covenant people and ensured his acquittal at the final judgment. For Paul, to think of the law in this way was to mistake the primary function of the law. On this, more later (especially 3:27–31)!

PRAYER

O Lord, when we confess our sin it is so easy to fall into the trap of thinking that others are more guilty than we, and that even if sinners, we at least have a reasonable excuse. Help us simply to pray, 'God have mercy on me, a sinner.'

To ALL WHO BELIEVE

But now...

Chapter 3 verse 21 marks a decisive shift in Paul's exposition. The 'But now' is not merely a literary flourish. The 'now' stands not merely in contrast to the preceding indictment. It also has an eschatological overtone: 'now' is the 'now time'. There has been a decisive shift in the course of events, in the course of history. This is the same 'now' that we meet elsewhere (5:9, 11; 8:1; 11:30–31; 1 Corinthians 15:20; 2 Corinthians 6:2). As these other references confirm, Paul's assumption is that the coming of Jesus, and especially his death and resurrection, has introduced a wholly new phase in the history of God's dealings with humankind. It is this 'now' which relativizes all that went before, including Israel's privileged position in relation to the other nations. Twenty-first-century readers of Paul's letters need to grasp something of this sense of total newness, for it was one of the distinctive features and driving forces behind the emergence and early spread of Christianity as a whole. In a word, the first Christians felt not only that a whole new epoch was opening before them, but also that this new epoch bore the character both of climax to all that God had intended from the beginning and of finality in the manner of God's dealings with Jew and Gentile.

The righteousness of God through faith

What launched this new epoch was the revelation of how God's righteousness was now to be perceived. 'The righteousness of God', we may recall, is the key motif for the letter as a whole. It denotes God's faithfulness to the commitment he has made. For Israel, who first recognized this character of God's dealings, that meant particularly his faithfulness to Israel, his commitment to maintain and sustain the people he had chosen. But now, without abandoning that first insight (3:1–6), Paul wants to affirm that this faithful God has made a similar commitment to all humankind, 'Jew first, but also Greek' (1:16–17). And since there is a universality in this claim, and since it looks beyond the initial choice of Israel, it cannot be limited to or by Israel's law. The law had served most effectively in regard to

Israel in the period when Israel alone was in view. But now the wider outreach of God's grace would be only restricted and constrained if funnelled through Israel's lawcode. This transformation in God's dealings had been predicted by the law and the prophets; Paul would probably have had scriptures like Isaiah 42:6–7 and 49:1–6 in mind.

The key revelation was that which the first believers had recognized in Jesus Christ, that Jesus marked the climax of God's purpose for humankind, and that God's gracious outreach (righteousness) was now available to all through Jesus. It was by turning to this Jesus in open trust that God's righteousness could now be accessed (v. 22). This phrase, 'through faith in Christ Jesus', is today often taken as 'through the faithfulness of Jesus Christ' (that is, in his death), with the role of human faith brought out in the following phrase, 'to all who believe'. It is more likely, however, that Paul turns to that aspect of his subject (what Christ did which makes the difference) in 3:24–26. Here the emphasis is on the alternative to the law as the means of human access to God's righteousness. That alternative is faith, trust in Christ, with the repeated emphasis ('to all who believe') in echo of the 'all' emphasis in 3:19–20: 'to *all* who believe'.

This latter emphasis is reinforced in verses 22–23. When Paul says, 'There is no distinction', he means primarily, 'There is no distinction between Jew and Greek' (10:12). The point is reinforced by another allusion to the account of Adam and Eve's failure in Genesis 3 (cf. 1:18–25). For in Jewish thought of the time, it was typical to see that primal failure in terms of a loss of share in the divine glory. Here Paul puts it in terms of both a falling short of the glory once shared, and also a falling short of the glory God had intended for humankind (cf. 1:23; 8:21). But once again, for Paul the Jew this affirmation of universal human sin means, primarily, Jew as well as Greek.

PRAYER

Grant, O Lord, that we experience for ourselves something of that first Christian sense of newness and wonder that your goodness should be bestowed so freely and so generously on all who trust in you, and to live our lives in that conviction and out of it.

15 ROMANS 3:24–26 (i)

REDEMPTION *in* CHRIST JESUS

Why so brief?

The link here is awkward (Paul simply carries on, 'Being justified…').
Consequently some have seen in these verses Paul's attempt to incor-
porate an earlier formulation, running from the beginning of 3:25 to
the beginning of 3:26: 'whom God set forth… in the forbearance of
God'. Such issues (whether Paul re-uses older confessional material)
are not usually of much consequence. Here, however, it might help
explain why Paul can treat the subject so briefly. For the brevity of this
paragraph is something of a puzzle. After the equivalent of two
lengthy chapters on his indictment, Paul responds in a mere six
verses (3:21–26). That must mean, presumably, that what he was
now saying was not controversial. What he needed to get over to his
readers was the inclusion of Jews within the indictment of all humanity; that was the controversial claim. That God had provided a solution to that plight in Jesus Christ and through his death was evidently
a bedrock conviction on which all believers were already united.

The problem which that leaves us is the difficulty of unpacking a
very compressed and summary statement. It also should remind us
that we must not weigh Paul's theology in terms of the number of
sentences he gives to it!

The gift of grace

Verse 24 is one of the classic statements of the gospel. It underscores
that God's justification and acceptance is a gift, by divine grace. This
last word, 'grace', is one of the words which Paul caught up from
a more ambiguous background to become a key statement of the
gospel. It characterized the gospel as the expression of God's spontaneous kindness and generous giving; and with the phrase 'as a gift'
added, the sense of God's acceptance as an undeserved favour is
doubled. Paul's concern thus far has been that when Israel claims a
favoured nation status, and when works of the law are introduced as
essential, then the gospel of God's free grace is compromised and
obscured. The generosity of God's grace is dependent on nothing
that humankind does or can do. Otherwise it would not be grace.

Several other points are worthy of note. One is that 'grace' does not denote simply a gracious disposition on God's part. For Paul, 'grace' is a dynamic concept: God gives grace; individuals receive grace. Another is that whereas the term was commonly used at that time in the plural—favours or benefactions done by someone, say, for a city—Paul uses it in the singular. For Paul, there is only one 'grace', the grace of God; every gracious act was only 'gracious' to the extent that it reflected the grace of God pre-eminently displayed in Jesus Christ. A third point deserving note is that in the world of the time, a favour typically was bestowed in expectation of its being reciprocated in some way. With Paul there is no room for the idea that God's grace can somehow be repaid. He does use the same word in describing human response, but always in the sense of 'thanks' (cf. 6:17; 7:25). Gratitude is the only appropriate response to grace.

Redemption in Christ Jesus

Paul adds a second metaphor to the law-court metaphor of 'justification, acquittal'—that of 'redemption' or 'liberation'. This would evoke images of the slave market, or of prisoners of war ransomed. In Deuteronomy, the Psalms and Second Isaiah, such language was often used of Israel's being ransomed from slavery in Egypt. Such imagery would evoke powerful emotions in members of the Roman congregations who were or had been slaves themselves (many of the first Christians would be in that position) or who identified with Israel's exodus as at the Passover. Those of us who have never been liberated need to pause and reflect on the power of the imagery.

'In Christ Jesus' is the first occurrence in Romans of a phrase much loved by Paul and distinctive of his theology (appearing over 80 times in his writings). It is difficult to gain a full sense of its significance, and it would be a mistake to narrow its significance to only one meaning. Here it seems to indicate being identified with Jesus in his decisive saving action on the cross and his life beyond. The experience of 'redemption' was, for Paul, bound up with the experience of being 'in Christ'.

PRAYER

O Lord our God, your grace reaches far beyond anything we could ever conceive, let alone deserve. We can do no more than acknowledge its richness, thank you for it and seek to live out of it. Help us so to do.

16 ROMANS 3:24–26 (ii)

GOD'S EXPIATION

Christ's death as sin offering

The summary statement of the gospel, on which Paul may start to draw in verse 25, focuses on the metaphor of Jesus' death as a sacrifice. This is clear above all from his use of the word *hilasterion* ('whom God set forth as a *hilasterion*') The word is used in the Pentateuch (the first five books of the Bible) quite often to denote the lid of the Ark, 'the mercy seat' as it was translated in the older translations (cf. Hebrews 9:5). The point is obvious from the context, particularly the addition of the phrase 'in his blood'. Paul was thinking of the fact that the lid of the Ark was where the blood of sacrifice was sprinkled on the Day of Atonement, as prescribed in Leviticus 16:14–15). This Day of Atonement ritual was particularly important: it was the only day and time when the high priest could enter into the Holy of Holies, where the Ark of the Covenant was; it was on that day and in that ceremony that the sins of the people as a whole were atoned for (cf. Hebrews 9:11–14).

The ritual of Leviticus 16 probably gives us some indication of how atonement was thought to work. The sins of the people were put on the head of one goat by the high priest laying his hands on it (16:21). Then it was abandoned in the wilderness, physically carrying away Israel's sins. That was one picture of atonement. In the case of the other goat we read that its blood was sprinkled on the *hilasterion* (16:15–17). Since the blood was the life of the animal (Leviticus 17:10–12), this presumably indicates that its life was being poured out before God. In other words, the animal identified with the sin of the people died; the sin of the people was poured away with the blood of the goat. That was another picture of atonement.

All this would be evoked by Paul's opening clause in verse 25. God provided Jesus as the place of atonement, or, by extension, as the means of atonement. The picture is of Jesus' death as the destruction of sin, of sin as a cancer cut out from the body of humankind, or as a kind of radioactive waste removed from the camp, taken far away and destroyed. Of course the imagery of sacrifice and sin-offering is a metaphor—just as the last two, more modern images are metaphors.

It would be idle to attempt to inquire more closely into the 'mechanism' of how Jesus' death actually 'worked' as *hilasterion*. What matters more is that relationship with God was effectively restored and the power of sin in human living effectively neutered.

Both just and justifier

God demonstrates his righteousness, for in his original commitment to Israel (3:3–5) he had provided a means for dealing with sin—that is, the sin offering, and particularly the Day of Atonement ritual. But what does Paul mean in his talk of God 'passing over [i.e. letting go unpunished] the sins committed in former times'? Does he mean that the sacrificial system had been a provisional way of dealing with sin and sinning, now superseded by Christ's sacrifice (cf. Hebrews 10:1–10)? Or does he mean that the effectiveness of the sin-offering (in removing the need for punishment) had been proved by the effectiveness of Christ's death as a sin-offering? It is very difficult to reach a conclusive answer on these questions.

It should not escape our notice, however, that we are back where we were at the beginning of the chapter. What is at stake in all this is the character of God, and particularly of God's justice (v. 26). God's justice can be celebrated, presumably because in dealing with sin, to punish, destroy and root it out, he displays his commitment against all that disfigures and corrupts his creation. The sacrificial system and what it expressed embodied that justice. But it also manifested God's commitment to redeem and uphold those who trusted in him—not simply to be just, but to justify. It is this commitment of God, manifested in creation, in the choice of Israel, and in Israel's sacrificial system, which Paul now sees expressed most fully in Christ and to those who trust in Jesus.

PRAYER

God of covenant grace, we confess our inability to understand why it is that you should be so concerned with sinners like us, and how it is that you are both just and justifier, both dealing with our sin and yet still calling us to yourself. But where we cannot understand, we can trust. And where we can trust, we can rest.

BOASTING IS EXCLUDED

The conclusion which Paul draws from his much-compressed state-ment in 3:21–26 is striking. In effect, he challenges his readers: any-one who has grasped the essence of the statement in 3:21–26 will see that it excludes 'boasting' (v. 27). Why this word, 'boasting', and why here? There is a long tradition to the effect that in using this word, Paul was thinking of the self-confidence of the pious individual, the boasting in self-achievement. But anyone who has been following Paul's development of his theme will recall the earlier use of the word in 2:17 and 23. There it summed up not the confidence of personal merit, but rather the confidence of the Jew as a member of God's chosen people, the boasting in God as Israel's God, the presumption that having the law indicated Israel's privileged position over other nations. It is evidently this boasting which Paul has in mind, as the following verses confirm.

In these verses he makes two points, summed up by the twin phrases, 'law of works' and 'law of faith'.

The law of works

In making his two points, Paul plays on the word 'law'. Such boasting is not excluded by 'the law of works'. Here he picks up the phrase ('works of the law') already used in summary way in 3:20. To under-stand the law in terms of 'works' is to think that the point of the law is particularly to be seen in commandments marking off Israel in its privileged position over against the other nations/Gentiles (2:17–24). But that would revive the old 'Jew and not Greek' distinction, whereas Paul's emphasis on 'all', 'Jew first but also Greek', leaps beyond that distinction (1:16–17; 3:22–23). This surmounting of the Jew versus Gentile distinction is evidently one of Paul's chief concerns. And it is this which Paul develops in verses 28–30.

The fact that Paul asks so abruptly, 'Or is God the God of Jews only?' (v. 29) shows clearly his train of thought. Evidently in Paul's mind, to affirm the importance of works (the law of works) is tantamount to affirming that God is the God of Jews only. This must mean that by 'works' Paul has in view the commandments of the law, by the keeping of which Jews most clearly distinguished themselves from Gentiles.

But that surely cannot be right. For Israel also confesses the *Shema*. Its basic creed is that God is one; there is only one God (v. 30). This was a confession which Jews recited every day (Deuteronomy 6:4). And that must mean that God is God of all nations, Gentiles as well as Jews. So his expectations of all humankind cannot be characterized by a law which is summed up in 'works' which serve precisely to divide Jew from Gentile. Paul affirms, on the basis of Israel's own creed, that there is a universalism which is integral to Israel's own identity. At this point he takes up the 'all nations' strand of Israel's heritage in passages like Genesis 12:3, Isaiah 42:6–7 and the book of Jonah.

The law of faith

The logic of confessing the one God as God of all, Gentile as well as Jew, implies that God deals with all alike. Justification/acceptance before and by God is by faith, for those who trust in him (v. 28), the circumcised by faith, and the uncircumcised through faith—the same faith, the same sort of trust (v. 30). There is a basic relation of dependence and reliance of human creature on divine Creator (cf. 1:21) which lies below any formal relation of rules and commandments.

But notice that in making this argument, Paul does not simply set faith and law in opposition, as though affirming faith meant disowning the law. It is 'the law of works', the law understood in terms of works (cf. 9:32), which he seeks to dismiss from the discussion. But the basic relation of humankind to God can also be described as 'the law of faith' (v. 27). That trust, that dependence and reliance, will also naturally and inevitably be expressed in regular patterns of conduct and responsibilities. As such, they can also be described as 'law', the law as lived by one trusting in God alone. This law is not Israel's alone, but for believing Gentiles too. This faith is the heart of living in accordance with God's will. That is why Paul can even affirm, to the surprise of many subsequent commentators, that faith does not make the law invalid; rather, it establishes the law (v. 31)!

PRAYER

Teach us, good Lord, what it means to believe—to believe not in a way which diminishes others but in a way which affirms others, to believe not in a way which diminishes you to the level of a tribal god, but in a way which truly acknowledges you as the Creator and God of all.

18 ROMANS 4:1-8

HOW GOD DEALS *with* HUMANS

What about Abraham?

An important test case for Paul's gospel was Abraham, for Abraham was the first and most highly regarded of the fathers of the nation. To him the promises had been given on which Israel's covenant with God was based. If the operation of God's righteousness in the case of Abraham could be clearly ascertained, it would provide a crucial precedent for those who claimed to be his heirs. Moreover, at the time of Paul's writing, Abraham was often regarded as the prototype convert, because, it was assumed, in abandoning Ur he had turned from idolatry (already implied in Joshua 24:2-3). So he could also be seen as the father of converts, and Paul could call him 'our forefather', where the 'our' must include his Gentile readers (v. 1).

In citing Abraham, Paul might seem to have played into his opponents' hands. For Abraham was remembered by Paul's Jewish contemporaries as the model of the devout Jew. Even as early as Genesis 26:5 it is affirmed that the promises (of seed, land and blessing for the nations) were given to him 'because Abraham obeyed my voice and kept my charge, my commandments, my statutes and my laws'. More frequently cited was the story of how Abraham had been tested and yet 'found faithful', with particular reference to the sacrifice of Isaac in Genesis 22. This was precisely the sort of attitude which the 'Jew' of 2:17 would have 'boasted' of, and which Paul summed up in terms of 'works of the law'. If 'works' was the issue, then Abraham would seem to have had something to boast about (v. 2).

Moreover, Paul would surely have been aware that his next key text—'Abraham believed God, and it was reckoned to him as righteousness' (Genesis 15:6)—was also cited by those who thought in terms of Abraham's works of faithful obedience. It was used, for example, in the Apocrypha, 1 Maccabees 2:52: 'When he (Abraham) was tested (in regard to the sacrifice of Isaac) he was found faithful, and it was reckoned to him for righteousness.' One of the most striking of recent discoveries is a similar line of exposition in a Dead Sea scroll first published in the early 1990s. It is known as 'Some of the Works of the Law' because it uses that very phrase to commend a number of the sect's distinctive rulings and practices, with the assurance that if the intended readers follow these works of the law 'it shall be reckoned to you as righteousness'.

Here again, then, Paul was skating on thin ice, as he set out to expound that key text differently (v. 3). The exposition will take up almost the whole chapter (4:4–21): first what it means that righteousness was 'reckoned' to Abraham (vv. 4–8), and then what it means that Abraham 'believed' (4:9–21), with 4:22 as the conclusion.

How does God 'reckon'?

Paul's starting point is that God's dealings with humankind are not like a contract between human equals (vv. 4–5), typified by fair wages for fair work. Because God is sovereign, the relation between Creator and creature is an unequal one, and depends wholly on the divine initiative and gift. A creature cannot warrant God's grace, and is wholly dependent on that grace from start to finish, a grace that is typified by God's reaching out to the disobedient and ungodly.

There is a strong tradition which deduces from verses 4–5 that the Jews of Paul's time thought of their own divine–human relationship in terms of working, as it were, to earn a wage. But that is unlikely: fundamental to Israel's sense of being God's people was the recognition that God had chosen a people quite without merit, a people enslaved by the Egyptians (e.g. Deuteronomy 7:7–8; 8:12–14). It is more likely that Paul is simply recalling the fundamental feature which distinguished God's dealing with humans from the way in which humans deal with one another. Its wholly gracious and even shocking character would be reinforced by the fact that 'justifying the ungodly' is just what a judge should *not* do (e.g. Exodus 23:7; Proverbs 17:15). Before such grace, the only possible response is one of trust.

Paul is able to substantiate his case (vv. 6–8) by noting another passage which speaks of God 'reckoning' (Psalm 32:1–2): God's forgiveness of David meant not reckoning David's sin and thus reckoning him righteous (that is, still held by God within the covenant bond, despite his sin).

PRAYER

Lord, we trust you, we trust in your grace; for if you are not gracious, then there is no hope for us; and if you are gracious, then all we can do is to trust in you and in that grace.

19

FAITH IS NOT DOING

But Abraham was circumcised!

Paul now declares his hand. The make-or-break issue for many Jewish believers concerned about Paul's mission to Gentiles was the issue of circumcision. That was why Paul had focused so closely on it in 2:25–29. Here Paul's exposition of Genesis 15:6 was in danger of being stopped short in its tracks. For any Jew listening to Paul's exposition of Abraham as the pattern for one who was reckoned righteous by God (accepted by God as covenant partner) would know at once the answer. Abraham had obeyed God's command to be circumcised and to circumcise the males of his household as part of his acceptance of God's covenant and promise (Genesis 17:9–14). So circumcision was part of the package for any Gentile seeking to share in the covenant grace of God.

Paul's answer was simple. Abraham believed and was reckoned righteous *before* he was circumcised: Genesis 15:6 comes some time (two chapters) before Genesis 17:9–14. He was reckoned righteous when he was still uncircumcised, still a Gentile (vv. 9–10).

For the Jewish believers who objected to Paul's line of argument, Paul's argument might have sounded not only simple but naïve. For them, it would be mistaken to try to divide up what was evidently a wholeness. The promises to Abraham were not a lot of separate promises, but all part of the one great promise, a promise repeated and reaffirmed throughout the history of the patriarchs—'the promise(s) to the fathers'. It was a promise with three parts: seed, land, and blessing for the nations (Genesis 12:1–3; 15; 17; 22:16–18; 26:2–6; 28:13–15; 35:11–12). The fact that the same promise was reiterated in a variety of circumstances and correlated with Abraham's various responses, including faith (Genesis 15:5–6), circumcision (Genesis 17:9–14), the offering of Isaac (Genesis 22:16–18), and law-keeping (Genesis 26:2–6), must mean that all the responses hang together. To separate them would be irresponsible.

For Paul, however, what was at stake was the most basic character of divine–human relationship. Genesis 15:6 showed that this relationship started on the human side from faith, that it was based on human trust in God's promise. Paul's concern was that to give equal focus to what followed from that faith (in this case, the circumcision in Genesis 17, or also, by implication, the offering of Isaac in Genesis 22) was to obscure the character of that relationship as possible only in terms of divine grace and human trust (4:4–5), and to confuse the character of faith as trust. Paul at this point was not concerned about what should follow from faith. His concern was to emphasize the only way in which the creature can relate to the Creator—the acceptance of divine grace.

Circumcision as a seal

The way to understand circumcision for Paul, therefore, was not (as we might say) as a sacrament through which God bestowed righteousness and acceptance into relationship with himself. Circumcision was rather a sign, and indeed a seal, of that relationship already established (v. 11). Here again, Paul was not saying anything new or revolutionary. For Jews, circumcision did not give them a place in the covenant with the Lord. As descendants of Abraham, they were already members of the covenant people. Circumcision was simply the first act of obedience by which that membership was demonstrated. Paul simply presses the point: circumcision is not to be confused with the thing itself (God's acceptance). It was, no doubt, the conversion of Gentiles to Judaism and the close relationship between their circumcision and their conversion which caused the confusion. Paul was seeking to clarify what was of first importance in understanding the relationship—that it was by grace through faith.

In so arguing, Paul did not intend to disparage circumcision, or to discourage his fellow Jews from practising it. He was content to affirm that Abraham was, of course, father of the circumcision (v. 12). He simply wanted to ensure that the fundamental character of that relationship remained clear—as one of trust from start to finish. If that point could be really grasped, then the issue of circumcision would be recognized as ultimately irrelevant (vv. 11–12).

PRAYER

Almighty God, there is always the temptation to make faith in you a complex matter of proper ritual and right confession. However it is that we see faith coming to appropriate expression, help us never to lose sight of the essential simplicity of trusting in you.

FAITH *in* GOD'S PROMISE

The character of divine promise

Now Paul turns to the second part of his exposition of Abraham's believing. Here he focuses on the link between Abraham's belief and the key word 'promise', a word which dominates this paragraph (vv. 13, 14, 16; also 4:20). It was a word which had only recently emerged into common speech; for example, it does not appear in the Greek translation of the Old Testament. But Paul seizes on it because it helps so well to make his case. As his further use of it in 9:4, 8–9 and 15:8 (as already in Galatians 3:14–29) clearly shows, the term 'promise' summed up for Paul the completely generous and unconditional nature of God's choice of and love for his people. Therefore, to understand rightly the character of God's dealings with Abraham as 'promise' is both to understand the wholly gracious character of these dealings, and to recognize that the fundamental response to such promise can only be faith, the unconditional acceptance of the promise.

The point is that when the promises of God to the fathers are seen as promises, then their character as grace and the human response as faith are safeguarded, and then the promises can be seen to apply also to Gentiles. For the law, which in the case of Abraham's physical descendants soon gathers round the promises, does not actually affect their character as promises. Rather, it is Abraham's faith which most closely fits to their character as promise. And faith can be exercised by Gentiles as well as Jews, and by Gentiles independently of the law which distinguishes Jews as Jews. This is the basic argument of verse 16.

So the promise must look beyond the nation of Israel

As part of this argument, Paul attempts to show that the promises to Abraham did not have in view merely his physical descendants or the promised land itself. In so doing, Paul makes clear that he was well aware that, for his people, the two chief strands of the promise to

Abraham were the promises of land (Genesis 12:7; 13:15; 15:18; 17:8) and of descendants (Genesis 12:2; 15:5; 17:4–5; 22:17).

But he was also aware that the idea of the land as 'inheritance' had already broadened out in Jewish thinking to embrace the whole earth—'from sea to sea and from the Euphrates to the ends of the earth' (Ecclesiasticus 44:21; cf. Matthew 5:5). He seizes on this larger interpretation of the promise to press home his more universal perspective on the promises (v. 13). The argument is the same as before: the promise came to Abraham through faith, well before the law came into the picture as the expression of God's unconditionally generous promise to Abraham. The grace/faith interdependence excludes conditions such as the law implies. If law is what determines the promise, then it is not faith alone (simple acceptance of the promise) and the promise ceases to be a true promise (v. 14). The business of the law is not to condition the character of grace or to determine the scope of grace. Its primary role is to define sin—a point which Paul makes repeatedly in this letter (3:20; 4:15; 5:13; 7:13).

In similar fashion, the other strand of the promise (descendants) must be seen on a far larger scale than simply Jews. The promise of seed did not have simply one nation in view, but 'many nations' (v. 17). Here Paul quotes directly from the Greek version of Genesis 17:5: scripture itself declares the promise that Abraham would become 'father of many nations'. But whereas traditional Jews may have thought only of converts or of near neighbours incorporated into the land of Israel, Paul seems to have merged this strand into the other strand of the promise to Abraham—the promise that the nations of the earth would be blessed through Abraham (Genesis 12:3; 18:18; 22:18; 26:4; 28:14). For Paul, the tie-in between recognition of God as the one creator God of all nations, and the character of God's promises to Abraham as promises, underlines the universal outreach of God's concern and that the only possible human response is faith (3:29–30; 4:17).

PRAYER

Lord, so many of our promises are self-seeking and grudging in character. Teach us to live as those whose guarantor is God and as ministers of your promises to the world.

FAITH IS TRUST

This is the third part of Paul's exposition of what 'Abraham believed God' (Genesis 15:6) means. It is the most profound description of faith in the Bible and gives a clear idea of what this faith is, that Paul opposes so resolutely to the alternative understanding of faith as necessarily requiring supplement or specific elaboration in particular 'works of the law' like circumcision.

Faith in God as Creator

Often missed is the way in which, at this point (v. 17), Paul goes behind his exposition of Abraham in Genesis 12ff. Here, Paul's point is, in effect, that the promise of God to Abraham (that he should be 'the father of many nations') cannot be adequately understood unless we appreciate that it is the Creator God who made that promise. That promise, in other words, is of a piece with God's most fundamental role of all: 'he gives life to the dead and calls things which have no existence into existence' (v. 17). This was the God in whom Abraham believed—not some tribal deity, or god of only one nation, but God the Creator.

The two clauses again evoke fundamental confessions of Israel. Jews had long celebrated God as the 'life-giver' (e.g. Nehemiah 9:6; Psalm 71:20). The second of the Eighteen Benedictions, one of the most ancient of daily Jewish prayers, confesses, 'You make alive'. The first Christians took up the same theme (in Paul, e.g. Romans 8:11; 1 Corinthians 15:45; 2 Corinthians 3:6; Galatians 3:21). Even more basic for a human being than an active relation with God is the fact of life itself. Even before he is God of Israel, or the God who justifies, he is God who gives life. That is the most fundamental miracle of all. Note how Paul picks up the theme again in 4:24.

The second clause was equally fundamental in Jewish thought. God's act of creation was quite often spoken of as an act of effective 'calling' (e.g. Isaiah 41:4; 48:13; Wisdom of Solomon 11:25), sometimes explicitly as creation *ex nihilo* (out of nothing) (e.g. 2 Maccabees 7:28). To confess that God is one, that there is only one God, is not simply to affirm that he is God of more than one nation; it is also to affirm that in the final analysis, God alone *is*. All other being is given existence by God. There is no other ultimate principle in the universe other than God. The promise to Abraham will be misunderstood unless it is set in the context of this more fundamental belief.

Faith as giving glory to God

This is why the human response can only be faith, the humble recognition of this most fundamental of facts, the grateful acceptance of the life given, and the confident trust in this promise-making, life-giving God. And of this faith Abraham is the great exemplar.

The point is that, so far as the promise of a son was concerned, Abraham had nothing to trust in for himself, nothing to hope for in himself or his wife (v. 18). His body was already dead, as was Sarah's womb (v. 19). But even though he was well aware of the impossibility of the promise in human terms, he hoped against hope and his trust in God did not weaken (vv. 18–19). That is the nature of the faith Paul commended—a faith which does not depend on human possibilities but looks solely to God; a trust which takes human inabilities into account and still trusts God.

A key phrase for Paul was that Abraham 'gave glory to God' (v. 20); that is, Abraham expressed that dependence on God which was the secret of human existence in the beginning and which humankind had abandoned (1:21). His faith was not simply in the God of covenant promise, but in the Creator. His trust was complete; he was wholly confident in God (v. 21).

And that is what faith is; that is what Genesis 15:6 means when it says, 'Abraham believed God'. That faith is more fundamental than any of Abraham's subsequent faithfulness, whether in regard to circumcision or to the offering of Isaac. That naked faith, lacking all support or supplement from anything human beings can do, is what God looks for in response to the gospel, from Jew as well as Gentile.

PRAYER

*Teach us, good Lord, the faith which trusts in you as the God who
gives life, as the God who brings into existence, as the God
who makes gracious promises for humankind simply to accept.
And enable us to live out of that faith, giving you the glory due.*

NOT JUST ABRAHAM, *but* US TOO

Reckoned to him for righteousness

Romans 4:3–22 has been Paul's attempt to elucidate what Genesis 15:6 means when it says, 'Abraham believed God and it was reckoned to him as righteousness' (4:3). Verse 22 rounds off the exposition: 'therefore (as understood in the way just explained) it was reckoned to him for righteousness'. That is to say, if we ask what God expects in terms of human response to his covenant grace and promise ('righteousness' indicating the fulfilment of obligation taken on by each partner in the covenant), then the answer is faith. When God's part is such unconditional generosity, faith is the only possible and appropriate human response. This is what the story of Abraham makes clear.

But that logic of divine grace does not apply to Abraham alone (v. 23). The key phrase, 'reckoned to him as righteousness', applied to more than Abraham. This was widely recognized at the time of Paul. What counted as fulfilment of obligation for members of the covenant included, for example, Phinehas's action to stem the plague (Psalm 106:31), and Abraham's faithfulness in the offering of Isaac (Genesis 22; 1 Maccabees 2:52). So Paul was doing nothing unfamiliar or underhand in applying the theological logic of the phrase to his own time. Scripture provided many indications of how divine/human relations should function. So too here.

For us who believe the gospel

Now, however, Paul has shown that the model supplied by Genesis' account of Abraham's believing and being counted righteous is to be understood differently. And that model fits very exactly to the situation of Paul's gospel preaching to Gentiles.

It was the same God in whom belief was called for. In verse 24, Paul deliberately echoes the description of God in 4:17. The God who 'raised Jesus from the dead' was the God who 'gives life to the dead' (4:17); the two phrases are synonymous (cf. John 5:21; Romans 8:11; 1 Peter 3:18). The resurrection of Jesus was precisely of a piece with God's giving life and calling into existence Isaac in the womb of Sarah. The faith called for by the gospel was just the same faith as Abraham had in the promise, the same fundamental trust regarding what was humanly impossible. That faith was faith in the Creator, the life-giver, a faith more fundamental than faith in God as Israel's God. For anyone who wanted to trust in the life-giving God, the manifestation of that power in the resurrection of Jesus was now its most obvious and climactic expression. Consequently also, faith in this God and this power as response to the good news of Jesus' resurrection was now the most fitting expression of that faith.

Paul implicitly presses home this last point by citing what is actually a summary of the gospel shared throughout the earliest churches. 'God raised him from the dead' was evidently one of the earliest credal-type affirmations of the first Christians (Acts 3:15; Romans 7:4; Galatians 1:1; 1 Peter 1:21). So too with the formulation, 'who was handed over because of our transgressions' (8:32; Galatians 2:20; Ephesians 5:2, 25). Worth noting at this point is the interwovenness of different aspects of Paul's gospel.

- Faith in Jesus is not something different from faith in God; faith in Jesus as Lord is trust that God raised him from the dead (10:9).

- The resurrection of Jesus is not to be separated from the death of Jesus. Here the emphasis is on the resurrection—the resurrection of Jesus as the act of the life-giving God. But Paul does not forget the exposition of 3:24–26: dealing effectively with human transgression in Christ's death (see Studies 15 and 16) is the other side of God's resurrection of Jesus from the dead. The pronouncement of justification, of divine vindication of the human, depends on both. Here justification is linked particularly to Christ's resurrection, partly because of the preceding argument, and partly because it is the resurrection of Jesus which demonstrates the success of Jesus' sacrificial death. In giving life to the dead Jesus, God calls into new existence from the non-existence of sin and death. To recognize and acknowledge that is the beginning of the justified life which shares in that new existence.

PRAYER

Blessed are you, O God, that you give life to the dead and call into being that which is not, that you raised Jesus from the dead and call into existence our feeble trust in you. Continue that work, we pray, in the world and in us.

23   ROMANS 5:1–2

The PRIVILEGES *of the* JUSTIFIED

The function of chapter 5 causes some discussion among specialists on Romans. Does it end the preceding exposition, or begin the next stage? Probably the answer is both, since Paul likes to sum up his argument in a way that provides a launch-pad for the next stage of the argument (cf. e.g. 3:20). In this case, the opening sentence (vv. 1–2) starts with what is obviously some sort of conclusion, before going on to elaborate the corollaries that can be drawn.

Justified—already!

Paul has now completed his main exposition of what he means by 'justification by faith' (3:21—4:25). So he can sum up on a triumphant note: 'Therefore, having been justified from faith...' (v. 1). Since the phrase is so heavily loaded with significance, we need to pause again to recall what Paul means by it. As the first appearances of the verb in 2:13 and 3:4 remind us, it is a metaphor drawn from the law court. To justify is to pronounce or acknowledge that a person has fulfilled the responsibilities which a particular relationship laid upon that person. To justify is to acquit. To justify is to declare righteous. Here it should be recalled that the verb 'justify' and the adjective 'righteous' come from the same root in both Hebrew and Greek.

In the case of the God/human relationship, the relation is of Creator to creature; or, in the case of Israel in particular, the covenant relation established through the promise to Abraham. Paul's point thus far has been to emphasize that, on the human side of the relationship, the human responsibility can only be faith, the trust of the powerless in the power of the life-giving God. God himself affirms such faith as righteousness (Genesis 15:6), as securing on the human side the bond with God which cannot be established or maintained otherwise. Hence the confident and rejoiceful note of the opening words—'having been justified *from faith*'. The Gentile believers to whom, especially, the letter is addressed were themselves evidence of how God's justification operates, since they had entered into this covenant relation with God simply by accepting the gospel which Paul preached (4:24–25).

The striking thing here is the tense Paul uses—the past passive, 'having been justified'. It was all well and good to use this tense for Abraham (4:2), since he belonged to the past. But here Paul is talking about his contemporaries. And earlier on, he had taken some care to maintain the overtone that justification is an ongoing activity of God (3:24, 26, 28; 4:5) with a view to future and final vindication at the final judgment (2:13; 3:20, 30). The point here must be, therefore, that Paul wishes to emphasize the decisiveness of the step of faith taken by his readers; what matters is that the new relationship with God has been firmly established. He will have enough to say on the outworkings of that new relationship in due course. Here it is the decisive character of its beginning on which he focuses.

The new relationship with God

The immediate consequence of God's acceptance is the character of the new relationship, summed up with three phrases.

First, it brings 'peace with God' (v. 1). 'Peace' here is not to be restricted simply to the Greek or modern idea of cessation of war. Nor should it be conceived as merely inner calm. The Hebrew concept of *shalom* had more the sense of 'well-being', including social harmony and communal prosperity (e.g. Ezekiel 34:25–31). This peace is the basis of mutual respect and fruitful cooperation.

Second, justification opens up unhindered 'access' to God. The metaphor is either that of the priest afforded full access to the immediate presence of God, or of the chamberlain granted immediate access to the royal presence. The metaphor would bring home to Paul's readers the amazing privilege they had been granted when God declared them 'justified'.

Third, this new relationship encourages an acceptable boasting (contrast 2:17, 23 and 3:27), a boasting in the hope that humankind's loss of glory (3:23) will be reversed in the fulfilment of God's plan for his creation. Paul here strikes the first note of a theme he at once elaborates (5:3–5). It will reach its climax in 8:17–25.

PRAYER

We praise you, O God, for the grace which reckons us
acceptable despite our sin. Forbid that we should boast in
anything of ourselves, ever more receive us into your presence,
and grant us your peace.

The HOPE *that* CAUSES NO SHAME

This is the first of Paul's two great expositions on the theme of hope in Romans. He had already linked it into his earlier talk of Abraham's faith: 'who against hope, in hope believed' (4:18). 'Hope' here clearly means that same confidence in God which faith expresses. In other words, the hope that Paul speaks of is quite different from the modern idea of hope, typically an uncertain expectation regarding the future ('I hope I may see you tomorrow, but I'm not at all certain about it'). In contrast, Paul understands 'hope' as confidence regarding the future.

What are the grounds for such a confident hope? One has already been given—the experience of being accepted by God, with the peace and access into his presence which that experience brought in its train (5:1–2). But Paul goes on to elaborate two others.

Hope as the product of suffering...

Paul has already rescued the concept of boasting from the negative overtones which had attached to it earlier (see Study 23 on 5:2). But he at once goes on to show how he has wholly transformed the concept of boasting.

The boasting he has in mind is a boasting also 'in our sufferings' (v. 3). That is a quite different kind of boasting from that in view in 2:17 or 3:27. There it was a boasting in privilege, a boasting in works. Boasting in suffering is the reverse of the other boasting. Such boasting is only possible if it does not rest in human status and benefit, if it rests only in God and not in any human strength. The weaker the human condition is recognized to be, the stronger the trust and confidence in God. This was something Paul had learned through his own experience (2 Corinthians 12:7–10), and ever since, the lesson had stayed with him that the cross is the unavoidable precursor of the resurrection (see also Romans 8:17–25). To boast in suffering in this sense has nothing masochistic about it. Rather, the boast is that the suffering drives the believer to ever greater reliance on God.

Paul spells this out in a typical sequence which brings out the value of suffering (vv. 3–4). Suffering produces 'patience, endurance, perseverance'—an important Christian virtue (e.g. 8:25; 15:4–5; 2

Corinthians 1:6). For Paul, this 'patience' was not simply a stoical acceptance of fate; rather it was the recognition that suffering has a positive value if accepted in the right spirit. That in turn produces 'character', that is, 'tested character' (the well known imagery of gold being proved or tested in fire). Which of us has not known the truth of this assertion, in the measured maturity of one who has suffered much but who has not allowed the suffering to embitter? Here is the outline of a Christian theology of suffering. Hope can be so confident because it rests not at all on human flourishing.

...and of experiencing God's love

The other ground of hope on which Paul fixes here is the experience of God's love 'poured out in our hearts' (v. 5). We should take seriously this affirmation of early Christian experience. What held people to this new faith to which they had been converted was evidently their rich sense of being loved by God (the metaphor is extravagant—God's love emptied out, as by an upturned pitcher, in their heart).

Also to be noted is the way Paul relates the gift of the Spirit to this experience. Reception of the Spirit was not a theoretical dogma to be believed in, a rational deduction from the step of faith (as is often the case today). The Spirit was encountered by Paul and others in and through the experience of being loved by God. In putting it thus, of course, Paul did not intend to indicate that such an intense experience of God's love is an invariable mark of the Spirit; but that is something to which we must return (see Study 42).

The point here is that hope was not understood as some sort of rational calculation. It surely grew out of belief in the gospel, trust in God's action in Christ as the demonstration of God's life-giving power. But it was given its force and its sustaining power by the experience of suffering as positively character-forming and of the Spirit as the medium of God's love.

PRAYER

Our hope is in you, O God, in you alone, and in nothing that we
can fully understand, and in nothing that we can do of ourselves.
If you spare us not from suffering, then grant us the suffering
that matures and grant us ever to know your love in our hearts.

25

The CHARACTER *of* SALVATION

God loves sinners

In summing up the wonder of God's justifying grace, Paul expresses himself in unforgettable imagery. He characterizes the human condition in a rising crescendo of stark terms—weak and ungodly (v. 6), sinners (v. 8), enemies (v. 10). Between them they cover and underline the serious state of humankind without God.

'Weakness' encapsulates the fragility of human existence. For all the accomplishments of human ingenuity and skill, our existence is simply weak before the powerful forces of nature. It is but as a moment of time in the sweep of history. Its moral inadequacies are captured in the word 'ungodly', recalling that word's headline use in 1:18 to sum up the indictment of humankind which followed in 1:18–32.

'Sinner' likewise is the most comprehensive term to describe the one who characteristically breaks or ignores God's law. What is of note at this point is the way Paul contrasts the sinner with the righteous or good person (vv. 7–8). The former contrast (righteous/sinner) was very familiar from the Old Testament (e.g. Psalm 1). But it often gained an unfortunate overtone—the self-conscious and confident 'righteous' looking down on those they regarded as 'sinners'. This was the contrast Jesus had criticized when he claimed that he came to call sinners, not the righteous (Mark 2:17).

Paul echoes something of the same criticism here. He uses the imagery of the martyr—an image familiar in Jewish circles, particularly since the Maccabean martyrs (2 Maccabees 7). For whom would you be willing to lay down your life? Paul implies that there is usually something unappealing about a 'righteous' person, that is, someone who is coldly determined to do what he or she regards as right, come what may. For a genuinely good person—that is, someone who, in contrast to the 'righteous', regards goodness as more important than rightness—some might indeed be willing to die. (Aristotle made a similar distinction between the man who is scrupulously just and the man prepared to make allowances.) But the measure of God's love is that Christ died for sinners—not righteous, not good, but breakers of

God's law. Paul, it should be noted, had no doubt that the death of Jesus was the expression of God's love, a conviction deeply rooted in the Christian gospel more or less from the first (cf. e.g. 2 Corinthians 5:18–21; John 3:16–17).

The third term, 'enemy', emphasizes still more the element of human responsibility—not just weak, not just guilty of (inadvertent?) sin, but hostile to God, opposed to God's purposes (v. 10; cf. 8:7).

The end is salvation

Paul is still thinking in terms of the grounds for Christian hope (5:3–5). Here (vv. 6–11) it is grounded in the unqualified and wholly generous character of God's love displayed in the death of Jesus. In making this latter point he uses one of his favourite phrases, 'how much more'. If God's initial outpouring of love was so uncalculating, how much more will be its complete manifestation! If already justified through the cross, the believer can be confident of full acquittal in the final judgment (v. 9). If already reconciled, despite being enemies, how much more is final salvation secure (v. 10). It is this confidence, in a process wholly of God and already manifestly begun in believers' experience, which makes it possible for Paul to 'boast in God' (v. 11, using the same verb as in 5:2–3).

To be noted here is the way in which Paul uses the metaphor of 'salvation'. The image is a medical one—of release from disease and restoration to health and wholeness. A common mistake in popular evangelism is to use it as a verb in the past tense. Christians are 'the saved' ('Are you saved, brother?') as though their salvation was already complete, as though in conversion they had been fully restored to health and wholeness. But Paul's most typical use of the imagery is of salvation as the final completion of the process, the restoration to wholeness as a life-long process, and believers as those who are in the process of being saved (1 Corinthians 1:18). So here (vv. 9–11), justification and reconciliation can speak of the initial acceptance by God, but salvation is still something to be looked forward to.

PRAYER

Gracious Lord, what are we that you should look on us in so kindly a way—weak, sinners, hostile even to what is for our own good? Draw us still to yourself in reconciling love, that we may be saved in the day of your wrath.

ADAM & CHRIST

It began with Adam

Human history as we know it began with the entry of sin into human experience. That is to say, to all intents and purposes there never was a time when humanity was without sin and death. To make this point, Paul turns once again (as in 1:18–23; 3:23) to the story of Adam in Genesis 2—3, with sin, in effect, in the role of the snake (even more clearly in 7:7–11), and death as the promised consequence of Adam's disobedience (Genesis 2:17). To understand his exposition here, we need to be clear on several points.

First, Paul is obviously well aware that the Hebrew term *Adam* literally means 'man, human being'. So what he says, he says about humankind as a whole. At this point he does not have in mind the distinction between 'man' and 'woman'. He was well enough aware of Eve's part in the Genesis account (2 Corinthians 11:3). But in Romans 5 it is 'humankind' as a whole, summed up in the 'one man', that he has in mind, and in the following paragraph he can sum up human transgression, sin and disobedience (cf. 5:6–10) by referring to that first act of human transgression, sin and disobedience described in Genesis 3.

This also means, second, that Paul was not thinking of such questions as, 'What was it like for Adam prior to the fall? Where did sin come from? Was death always part of God's purpose in creating humankind?' What he draws from the Genesis story at this point is simply the fact that sin and death are now real and unavoidable factors of human existence. The insight is important: there are many influences on human existence which can be escaped or moderated, but no human being can escape the power of death or the power of sin. That is the whole point and purpose of religion—to offer a counter to these all-too-real realities of human experience.

The role of the law

Paul follows out the story as told in the first five books of the Bible. Following from the first father of humankind (Adam), and skipping over the patriarchs, the next major event was the exodus and the giving of the law at Sinai (v. 13). Paul's treatment is slightly confusing: the law reveals sin in its character as transgression; the law embodies the divine command which human sin breaks. Thus he can speak (v. 14) of Adam's failure as a 'transgression' (of the divine command of Genesis 2:17), while recognizing the conundrum: no law, no transgression; and yet death nevertheless 'reigned from Adam to Moses'.

The third point of clarification, then, is that sin is something more fundamental than the transgression of explicit commands. It is experienced by humankind, as Adam experienced the snake, as a power which plays upon human weakness, and entices individuals to break the known instructions of God. Paul elaborates the point in 7:7–13.

A fourth point of clarification is that Paul therefore may be said to teach a doctrine of 'original sin', but not of original guilt. All are prey to this power in their lives (sin); but guilt can be spoken of only when there is a deliberate transgression of known law. All humankind die, we may say, as a result of weak and sinful humanity turning its back on God (the only power that can fully counter human weakness); but humankind is not held responsible for some original sin. In that sense, all die because all sin (5:12); their own transgression reinforces the power of sin and makes death, as the consequence of sin, ever more inescapable.

Adam, the 'type' of Christ

The final clause clarifies further what Paul is doing. He is thinking of Adam as one who typifies humankind as a whole. But he typifies still more the other one man who makes a difference—Jesus Christ. Between these two figures Paul can sum up the whole destiny of the human race. As Adam marks the beginning of human destiny in thrall to sin and death, so Christ marks the beginning of human destiny delivered from these powers. This is the comparison and contrast Paul goes on to develop in the next section. Thus even Adam, when set within the sweep of the divine purpose, can be a figure of hope.

PRAYER

*Lord God, it is all too easy for us to be caught up in the little
things of everyday life and to forget the big picture. It is so easy to
become oppressed by the reality of sin and death and to forget that
behind even these powers, you stand, and your overall purpose.
Lift up our eyes to you.*

27 ROMANS 5:15–21

HOW MUCH MORE

Grace versus trespass

The comparison and contrast between Adam and Christ is sustained as Paul, in one of his purple passages (vv. 15–19), attempts to express the wonder that he felt when considering the grace of God in Christ.

The comparison lies in the fact that the two men can similarly be said to represent humankind as a whole, or, alternatively, the two possibilities and destinies open to humankind. What marks them out is the fact that a single ('one') action of each can be regarded as triggering off and characterizing a whole epoch, and that they can stand for and typify the destinies of 'all/the many' within these epochs.

The two men, their two epochs and the two resultant destinies are characterized by a set of contrasts: 'trespass to death'/'gift of grace' (v. 15); 'sin/gift', 'judgment to condemnation'/'free gift to justification' (v. 16); 'trespass to death'/'grace and gift of righteousness to life' (v. 17); 'trespass to condemnation'/'righteous act to righteousness of life' (v. 18); 'disobedience to sinners'/'obedience to righteous' (v. 19). There is a good deal of rhetorical flourish here, and Paul uses a number of words which he rarely calls on elsewhere to achieve the effect. Consequently it is more important to feel the impact of the cumulative contrasts than to attempt to discover distinctive nuances in the varied vocabulary. This applies to Paul's use of 'the many' and 'all' as more or less synonymous: Paul is not so much thinking of Christ's action accomplishing universal salvation, as trying to bring out the fact that his overall picture of human history covers everyone.

The extent of the contrast is brought out still more clearly by the extravagance of his language: 'how much more' the grace of God 'overflowed' to the many (v. 15); the judgment 'from one' is to condemnation, but the free gift is 'from many trespasses' to justification (v. 16); 'how much more the abundance of grace' (v. 17). Here again, as in 5:1–5, it is the wonder of what Paul had experienced for himself which could only express itself in hyperbole—the 'so much more' of grace countering his all-too-clear consciousness of sin still battening on his weakness. At points like this, we need to recall that worship requires the exuberance of imagery and poetry that doctrine would rather shy away from.

Death or life

In the final two verses Paul sums up the cast list which has to be called to account if the human drama is to reach a successful conclusion. In so doing, he is, as so often, setting the agenda for what he intends to cover in the following chapters—roughly speaking, sin (ch. 6), law (ch. 7) and death (ch. 8).

The role indicated for the law in 5:20 would come as a shock for any more traditional Jews in the Roman churches. Far from serving as a solution or remedy for sin, Paul implies that it came in as an aide to sin. This is often taken to imply that Paul saw the law as, equally with sin and death, an evil power hostile to humankind. Paul recognizes that his language could give rise to such misunderstanding, and in chapter 7 he goes out of his way to correct it (7:7–25). It is more likely, then, that he is rhetorically emphasizing the role and consequence of law already indicated in 5:13: the law makes it clear when God's will has been transgressed; in that sense it 'increases' the trespass. But the objective is actually to ensure that the extent of sin and its true character are fully exposed (cf. 7:13), in order that it may be fully dealt with, in order that humanity's real enemies (sin and death) can be comprehensively banished.

The problem is that death, which might otherwise simply have been a stage in human existence, becomes something fearful and repelling when it is allied to sin, when it is sin's triumph ('sin reigned in death'). That is the state and end for those in the epoch of Adam. But Christ's obedience to death provides a more than adequate counter to the rule of sin in death; it opens up a new epoch in which death has been overcome by life, and so the power of sin, 'the sting of death' (1 Corinthians 15:56), has been nullified (cf. 6:7–9). Here again, the 'how much more' is evident in the thought of grace abounding to sinners to eternal life (vv. 20–21).

PRAYER

'Grace abounding to sinners.' How can we begin to appreciate the depth and richness of your grace to us poor humans? Deliver us, we pray, from the power of sin and death, so that we too, by your grace, may rejoice in eternal life through Jesus Christ our Lord.

28   ROMANS 6:1-4

You Have Died *to* Sin

So don't live in it any more

With the central line of his argument completed and his vision shared of God's grace in its universal scope embracing all history, Paul can now turn to some key clarifications. The first of these is whether sin can have a continuing place in the Christian experience of discipleship. The argument is simple and beguiling. Paul has implied that when sin increases, the grace of God increases to counter it (5:20). If God's grace is most clearly evident in his outreach to sinners and his reconciliation of enemies (5:8, 10), then sin has a good side, since it results in more grace (v. 1)! If God's grace is forgiveness, then should we not expand his business by increasing our call on that forgiveness? This, we may recall, was the slander which had been brought against Paul, to which he refers in 3:8, and to which he has not so far been in a position to mount an effective reply.

Paul's answer is an instant and outright rebuttal—'Certainly not!' (v. 2). Anyone who thinks like that has simply failed to recognize how radical and far-reaching is the transition from the epoch stamped by Adam's transgression to the epoch stamped by Christ's gracious act. That transition is nothing less than the transition from death to life. Those who have responded to the gospel have made that transition; the old way of living under the rule of sin and death has been left behind. In effect they have died to sin; so how can they still live in it?

Curiously, some have taken Paul's response as woodenly as those who objected to his gospel of grace (v. 1). They argue that Paul must be taken literally here: the Christians to whom Paul writes should have accepted that they had literally died to sin, that is, were incapable of sin and so were now perfect. How any could affirm this in view of the second part of the chapter (6:12–23) is something of a puzzle. But Paul's thought still runs with the extravagant language of 5:15–21. His readers need to appreciate that a decisive step has been taken; a decisive shift in the powers ruling their lives has taken place. The shift from one epoch to another is not yet complete; it will only be so when death has had its final say in physical death and they are made fully alive in resurrection (cf. 1 Corinthians 15:20–22). This will become steadily more clear as his exposition develops through chapters 6—8; 6:2 is only the opening statement.

Died with Christ to walk in new life

The initial development (vv. 3–4) already gives the most important clue. The death they have died is a death 'with Christ'. Here Paul strikes the first note in one of the profoundest themes in his theology —the theme marked regularly in his thought with the phrases 'in Christ', 'with Christ' and 'through Christ'. Faith in God, in Christ, in the gospel, which Paul has expounded so powerfully in chapter 4, is a handing over of individual life to be bound up with Christ, both in his dying and in his resurrection life. It is that intimacy of personal relationship with this Christ which gives Paul's exhortation its confidence.

To give more substance to the talk of dying to sin with Christ (cf. 6:7–11), Paul recalls the imagery of their baptism. They had all, no doubt, been baptized in(to) the name of Christ (cf. 1 Corinthians 1:13). They should see in that the symbol of their being immersed into the reality of Christ himself. The term ('baptize') itself denoted sinking below the surface, drowning indeed. Paul picks up the imagery: they were drowned in Christ, they were baptized into his death (v. 3).

Paul does not take up what subsequently became an important part of baptism's symbolism—the emergence from the water as a symbol of resurrection from the dead. He focuses only on the imagery of sinking into the water as an imagery of burial with Christ (v. 4). Of course, the 'with Christ' means that the effect of his resurrection can also be experienced in their ongoing living, at least in a preliminary way. Christ was also raised, and for those identified with him, that means the possibility of walking in newness of life.

PRAYER

How is it that we who have received such grace can still transgress, sin and disobey? And yet we do. Forgive us, Lord, and grant us the grace not simply of your death but also of your resurrection, that we may not simply be forgiven but may also express your new life in ours.

The EFFECT of CHRIST'S DEATH

The end of sin's power

The first elaboration of the primary theme of 'died to sin' (6:2) was Paul's exposition of the symbolism of baptism (6:3–4). The second elaboration uses still bolder images.

In a very compressed sentence, Paul takes up the imagery of the broken ends of a bone being fused together to form a new whole ('united', v. 5, NRSV). The two ends in mind are the 'we' of Paul and his audiences in Rome, and what he calls 'the very likeness', first of Christ's death and then of his resurrection. What he means by 'the very likeness' is not clear. It cannot refer to the historic facts of Christ's death and resurrection themselves; otherwise Paul would not have used the slightly distancing term 'very likeness of'. Nor is it likely that he is thinking again of their baptism, for the verb tense he uses (perfect tense) indicates that the process of the two ends of the broken bone growing together results in the two ends being permanently fused as one. To envisage baptized Christians as still in the baptismal water, permanently drowned, would be odd indeed! Most likely, then, he is thinking of the effect of Christ's death in their lives, in their death to sin (6:2). That effect is a permanent one in shaping the life of believers in their ongoing relation to sin.

A very striking feature of Paul's theology thus begins to become clear. Paul did not think of believers' dying with Christ as a single event in their conversion (or baptism). Rather the step of faith was an engagement with Christ in his death which was to last their whole life through. That was why Paul elsewhere could say, 'I have been crucified with Christ' (Galatians 2:20), where the tense is the same, indicating not that he had once been crucified with Christ and then been taken down from the cross, but that he had once been nailed to the cross with Christ, and was still hanging there! This sense of an ongoing sharing in Christ's sufferings and death as an integral part of the process of salvation was evidently important for Paul (see also 8:17). Here we should simply note that the future tense used in the second half of verse 5 confirms that, for Paul, the equivalent integration of believers into the likeness of Christ's resurrection lay still in the believers' future.

The other bold variation on the metaphor of death with Christ is the equivalent conviction that what was crucified with Christ was 'our old self', with a view to 'the body of sin' being done away with or rendered ineffective (v. 6). 'The body of sin' obviously denotes life lived in the body by those still in the epoch of Adam and still under the power of sin (5:21a), conditioned by human weakness and dominated by the compulsion to satisfy human appetite (cf. 6:12; 7:5). The implication is that doing away with that old condition is itself a vital aspect of the process of salvation, not an already accomplished fact.

As Christ died and lived again...

The remainder of the paragraph fills out the comparison being drawn with Christ's death. Paul picks up what might already have been a popular saying, along the lines of 'Death ends all relationships, cancels all debts'. The irony of sin's power is that the death it brings about (5:21) also ends its reign: a dead body is no longer responsive to its allurements (v. 7). The truth of this is seen in Christ's death and resurrection: neither sin nor death has any more hold on him (v. 9). His death was once for all, finished and done; the life he now lives is no more subject to death (v. 10).

The point is that this pattern set by Christ (death as freeing from sin, life as unending before God) is the pattern also for those united with Christ through faith. The only difference is that the pattern is already completed with Christ. For the believers, however, it has only begun: they have already 'died with Christ'; they believe that they will also 'live with him' (v. 8). So, whereas for Christ the dominance of sin and death is complete, for believers the grip of sin is broken, but the rule of death has still to be played out in the believers' own dying, when it will be followed by resurrection with Christ. In short, the process of salvation once begun has yet to be completed. In the meantime, the believer's responsibility is to live as one who has 'died to sin' and in the light of the coming resurrection (v. 11).

PRAYER

We praise you, O God, that we see in Christ's death and resurrection the basis for our own hope and the pattern for our own daily living. Enable us ever more to live as dead to sin and alive to God in Christ Jesus.

The CHANGE *of* LORDSHIP

Sin should have no more say in your lives

Paul has reminded his readers of two great facts which should determine their present lives. One is the death and resurrection of Jesus Christ. By his death he has escaped and thus broken the power of sin; by his resurrection he has escaped and thus broken the power of death (6:7–10). The other fact is their own identification with Christ through faith (6:2–6, 11). In so identifying with him, they identify with his death and new life; they have begun to share in its outcomes. So they no longer need to acknowledge any power of sin in their own lives, and the fear of death is likewise broken.

That might seem to be all that needs saying. But the reality of life still to be lived in this world, pre-resurrection, as we might say, had still to be confronted. And the process of salvation, while decisively begun, had still a long way to go in the ongoing lives of believers: identification with Christ's death had still to work through in the dying away of 'the old self' (6:3–6); they should act 'as those alive from the dead' (v. 13), even though resurrection with Christ still lay in the future (6:5, 8).

The resulting issue has a long history in Christian thought—the issue of Christians who don't live like Christians. In early centuries it was often characterized as the problem of post-baptismal sin; it was one of the reasons why catechumens so often delayed baptism till their final days, so that their baptismal purity would not be besmirched by subsequent sin. That way of posing the issue probably gave too much weight to the significance of baptism, and sometimes created afresh the problem, posed in 6:1, of those baptized thinking that they could do anything without its being reckoned as sin.

Today we might pose the issue in terms of achieving the right balance between giving the proper weight to what God has already accomplished in Christ and ensuring a proper sense of moral responsibility on the part of believers. What is evident from this passage is that Paul confronted the same issue in similar terms: confidence in what God has done and will do must be matched by active resistance to sin's continued claims and an actively sustained commitment to

God. The balance is nicely caught in the opening words of verse 14: 'sin will not exercise lordship over you'—a mixture of promise and encouragement.

Under grace; so live

Paul's exhortation provides a fuller insight into how he understood the power of sin to operate. It worked through the weakness of the human body, playing with human desire and appetite (v. 12). The word 'desire' can also mean 'lust'; the effect of sin, we may say, is to transform desire into lust. In verse 13 he thinks of human existence in terms of its various 'parts, members', made up of a whole sequence of particular acts and relationships. These too in their particularities have to be deliberately handed over to God, otherwise they all too easily fall prey to the insidious effects of sin, of greed and self-concern.

To be noted also is the balance Paul achieves in the tenses used in verses 12–13), both present and the Greek aorist (past tense). The former indicates an ongoing obligation, a resolution in act which has to be regularly repeated: 'Stop giving sin control of your daily living'. The latter indicates a decisive act—'give God control of yourselves'— although, since it is an exhortation to those already baptized into Christ (6:3), presumably Paul again has renewed commitment in mind; in that sense, conversion has to be every day, in daily renewed moral earnestness.

Verse 14 recalls the division of human history into its two epochs (5:12–21). The change of lordship can be characterized as 'not under law but under grace'. The former characterizes human existence in Jewish terms. The law here presumably refers to the two roles Paul has so far ascribed to it in this letter—the first as making conscious of sin (3:20) and as the measure of human sinfulness (2:12–16); the second as reinforcing Israel's set-apartness from the (other) nations. Simply to stand under judgment (2:12) or under a deceptive presumption (2:17–29) is no longer where believers stand. They stand now under the rule of grace, the grace of God the life-giver.

PRAYER

Help us to appreciate more and more clearly what it means to be no longer 'under law' but 'under grace', and grant us the daily renewed commitment and day-to-day resolve to live out our lives in all their parts in that awareness.

31   ROMANS 6:15–23

The TWO SLAVERIES

Why 'slavery'

As Paul had elaborated the starting claim ('died to sin') in a sequence of vivid images (6:3–6), so now he elaborates his exhortation to live 'as alive from the dead' (6:13) by an extended use of the imagery of slavery. In a world where slavery was taken for granted, and where a large proportion of the citizens of Rome were themselves slaves, the force of the imagery would be fairly obvious. And since manumission (setting a slave free) was also a common feature of the slave system, it excited the longing for freedom on the part of the typical slave and provided another obvious metaphor for religious conversion. Many of the members of the Roman churches would have been either slaves or freedmen and freedwomen.

All this makes Paul's use of the imagery here the more striking. For we might think that the obvious application was to characterize coming to faith in Christ as itself a liberation, with believers spoken of as freedmen and women. And Paul does indeed make use of the powerful metaphor of liberation (vv. 18, 22), though its stronger use comes in 8:2, 21 (cf. Galatians 2:4; 4:22–31; 5:1, 13). But instead of seeing faith here simply as being set free, Paul describes the transition of conversion as a change of master, as a change from one slave master to another. Having been slaves of sin, they have become slaves of righteousness (vv. 16–18, 20). Having been slaves of uncleanness and lawlessness, they should have become slaves of righteousness which results in consecration (v. 19).

This somewhat surprising feature of Paul's exhortation actually helps bring home something that Paul saw as basic to humankind and that had lain behind the indictment of 1:18–32. This is the fact that human beings cannot themselves gain mastery over the forces that determine their lives. By the very fact of the way they are constituted, they will always be in a condition of dependency. They will always be slaves, unable to determine their own destiny, slaves to whatever they 'obey', whatever they give control of themselves to (v. 16).

So here, liberation from these lesser things, from the power of sin, is best seen not as liberation from all restraint, but as transfer to a different slave owner—in fact, as a reversion to the dependency of creature on Creator, in which relationship alone the human creature can find its true fulfilment. In other words, the exhortation here can be re-expressed in terms of, 'Be true to yourself, to your own God-given nature, to your own best interest'.

The fruit of the two slaveries

The contrast of the two slaveries is most clearly seen in their outcomes. In the one case, the imagery well serves Paul's repeated point about the close tie-up between sin and death. For as was well known, there were many harsh and cruel slave owners. The death of a slave from ill-treatment was not uncommon and would not necessarily be remarked upon, since slaves were expendable. Sin is such a slave-owner: it devalues the person, frees them from moral responsibility (v. 20), abuses their true dignity ('things of which you are now ashamed', v. 21), and pays no wages other than death (v. 23).

In contrast, enslavement to God produces a consecrated life which causes no shame (v. 22), and the end product is eternal life, with the power of death left far behind (v. 23). This contrast, first clearly drawn in 5:21, is here repeated as a major feature of Paul's exposition in chapters 5—8 (see also 8:2, 6, 10; and 8:38!). The contrast is also between 'wage' and 'free gift' (v. 23; cf. 4:5). Once again it is generosity which marks divine–human relationship; without it, the relationship simply could not be sustained.

Verse 17 is worth a further note. What Paul means when he says, 'to which or whom you were handed over as a pattern of teaching' is unclear. Most take it as referring to some creed or code of conduct given to converts at their baptism or early training. But for Paul the term 'type' ('pattern') almost always has a personal reference (as in 5:14). So the reference here is probably to Christ himself as providing the pattern for Christian living.

PRAYER

Lord, there are so many things and prospects which attract and
entice us to give ourselves in their pursuit and service, but whose
end, we know, is destructive. Help us to recognize the character
of the moral choices we have constantly to make,
and help us to choose what is right.

FREED *from the* LAW

Divorced by death

Having tackled the subject of sin, whether it should still have any say in the Christian's life, Paul turns to law, the second member of the triumvirate of 5:20–21. He starts with an analogy which has caused endless bewilderment (vv. 1–3). The basic parallel is clear enough. A woman who is a wife is bound by the law of marriage. Legally she is not free to live with another man while her husband is alive. But if her husband dies, she is free from that law, and can marry another man without penalty.

The parallel at first is straightforward. The woman is the believer. The death of the first husband frees her to belong to the new man, Christ (v. 4). But then the problems arise. Who is the first husband? Sin? But Paul has nowhere spoken of *sin* as having already died. Quite the contrary: sin is the other master to whom allegiance must now be denied (6:15–23). 'The old self' (6:6)? That makes better sense, since a crucial part of the salvation process described in chapter 6 is precisely the doing away with the old self (6:6; 7:6). But then we have the awkward personality split between the Christian as the wife and the Christian's old self as the husband. Still, maybe we could live with that in view of the personality split envisaged in 7:14–25. Even so, we're still not out of the woods, since in verse 4 the death died is that of Christ. So, the death of Christ is equivalent to the death of the first husband, but Christ is also the new man/husband in the believer's life.

Confused? Of course! But don't treat the analogy as an allegory with a point-by-point explanation. Only two things really matter: first, that a death ends relationships; and second, that in some sense the believer is free from the law. It is the latter which explains why Paul introduces the awkward analogy. For it is precisely the role of the law in all this which Paul is going to try to clarify in this chapter.

Free from the letter

With verses 5–6, Paul leaves behind the somewhat confusing analogy of verses 1–4 and speaks more plainly. And he does so in a way which sums up both the human plight in relation to sin, death and the law

(v. 5), and the freedom from the law which the new life in Christ entails (v. 6). In fact, verses 5–6 serve as a sort of headline for the rest of chapter 7 (v. 5) and for the main thrust of chapter 8 (v. 6).

Verse 5 is one of the clearest statements of how Paul envisages the power of sin exercising its death-achieving grasp on humankind. The *flesh* indicates the scope of human weakness—the weakness of the physical, vulnerable to sickness and decay; the weakness of the human being dependent on the satisfaction of all-too-human appetites. The problem is that *sin* is the power which transforms desire into lust and thus secures and maintains its hold on the human condition—the grip of an insatiable appetite, of a habit out of control. In this, sin finds a useful tool in the *law* which arouses these desires—the attraction of the forbidden (7:7–11). The end product is *death* (cf. 5:20; 6:23). As the end product of sin, death obviously denotes destruction, the end of that process of physical and moral decay, the end result of a life given over to undisciplined habit.

It is from this condition that the death of Christ, and the Christian's identification with Christ in his death, have delivered the believer. They have been freed from that vicious cycle of sin feeding on the weakness of the flesh to produce death. That vicious cycle has been replaced by the virtuous cycle of Spirit and life (v. 6).

Here (v. 6) Paul puts it in terms of freedom from the law, since it is the way sin uses the law to stir up 'the sinful passions' which Paul has so much in the forefront of his mind. But verse 6b makes it clear that he has in mind the law in its character as the 'old letter'; that is, the slavery from which the believer has been delivered. And by the 'letter', Paul has in mind (cf. 2:29) the law in its visible and literal expression. It is freedom from the rules which counted for so much among his fellow Jews that Paul is thinking of here. The contrast is, again, not freedom from servitude (cf. 6:16–23), but freedom for a different service, the new life of the Spirit. To elaborate that claim will be the climax of his exposition, in chapter 8. For the time being, it is the continuing role of the law which he will go on to explain further.

PRAYER

Almighty God, the death of Christ works for us in ways that we can hardly begin to understand. Grant us to know more and more the freedom from the old way of life determined by sin and death and more and more to experience the new life of the Spirit.

In DEFENCE *of the* LAW

The law's true role

As with chapter 2, the logic of Paul's argument seems to be pointing inexorably to an inescapable conclusion. There, it was that being a Jew and circumcised was of no benefit whatsoever. And Paul had to deny it: however logical that conclusion appeared, it was wrong (3:1). Here, his argument has seemed to denigrate the law pretty thoroughly: it was the ally of sin and death (5:20); it was the antithesis of grace (6:14–15); it was a form of enslavement to which believers had died and from which they had been liberated (7:4–6). Here again the conclusion seems inescapable: the law is an evil power, or indeed simply another manifestation of the power of sin. And as before, Paul does not duck the issue: does it not follow from all that he has said 'that the law is sin' (v. 7)?

Subsequent Christian thinking has often followed the same logic and concluded that Paul was implacably opposed to the law. In the second century, Marcion drew and pressed home this conclusion by arguing that the God of Christianity was quite different from the God of the Old Testament and that Christianity should have nothing to do with the Old Testament and its law. Later theologians have not been so radical, but still the impression is deeply rooted in Protestant theology that Paul was throughly opposed to the law. It is very important, therefore, to note that Paul himself raises the question (whether the law is irredeemably flawed)—only to reject it!

His first point is to recall what he has stressed several times already—that the function of the law is to define sin and to bring awareness of sin (v. 7; also 3:20; 4:15; 5:13). The trouble is that sin makes use of that function and abuses it. We have already characterized sin as that power which turns desire into lust. Here Paul elaborates that very point. Sin, as we might say, is that power which turns consciousness of sin into enticement to sin. If that point can be grasped, then the function of the law can more clearly be distinguished from such consequences and that function defended. The law is, after all, the law of God, and is thus 'holy and just and good' (v. 12). Indeed, in one sense the achievement of sin in bringing about lust and disobedience through the law strengthens the law's function, for in achieving corruption and death the 'utterly sinful' character of sin is demonstrated (v. 13). The enticement of sin in conjuring up the attractiveness of a life devoted to self-satisfaction is always short-term; the end product is very different (5:20; 6:23; 7:13).

Echoing Adam again

Paul develops his case here by once again looking back to the story of Adam in Genesis 2—3 (cf. 5:12–19). In this case more clearly than before, he reads that story as a mirror of (univeral) human experience (we recall again that the Hebrew term *adam* = 'man'). As the Jewish apocalypse written a generation later put it: 'Each of us has been the Adam of his own soul' (2 *Baruch* 54:19). Paul is clearly thinking in particular of God's commandment to Adam that he could eat from every tree in the garden, including, by implication, the tree of life (Genesis 2:9, 16–17), but that he must not eat of the tree of the knowledge of good and evil, 'for in the day that you eat of it you shall die' (Genesis 2:17). That was humankind's condition of dependence, dependent on the Creator for moral consciousness and guidance. But sin (the snake) made it sound as though God was keeping something back from Adam, that Adam could be free from that dependence, could indeed be like God, 'knowing good and evil' (Genesis 3:1–5). That, says Paul, was the root of human failure.

As did others of his time (cf. James 1:14–15), Paul sums up that root in terms of 'desire'. God's command to Adam in the garden was a form of the tenth of the Ten Commandments: 'You shall not covet'. Sin (the snake) used that command to stir up that very covetousness (v. 8)—the desire for moral independence. The result was indeed independence from God. But such independence meant death, not life (vv. 9–10). For the implication of the warning of Genesis 2:17 and its result—banishment from God's presence (Genesis 3:22–24)—is that life is to be found in the presence of God. Verse 11 echoes the woman's (Eve's) sad complaint: 'Sin deceived me' (Genesis 3:13).

PRAYER

How easily we are deceived, O God, by the superficial and the temporary. How easily we deceive ourselves and try to shield our consciences from the true nature of our life-and-death situation. Help us to recognize sin for what it is.

34 ROMANS 7:14–20

The DIVIDED 'I'

I am fleshly

In his defence of the law, Paul's argument thus far has been fairly straightforward: the law is not sin; its true function (defining sin and making us conscious of sin) has been perverted by the power of sin; the real culprit is sin itself (7:7–13). But the problem goes deeper. Why is it that sin is able to use the law in this way? Why is it that knowledge of what is good and evil becomes enticement to evil? Why is it that desire is corrupted into lust? Why do we covet in the first place? The problem, Paul now goes on to indicate, lies with ourselves. The law is of God, but I am of the flesh (v. 14).

We need to pause here to grasp more fully the meaning of this key term in Paul's thinking. By 'flesh', Paul does not mean simply the physical structure of human existence. He implies more than that: as with Isaiah 31:3, flesh denotes human weakness (cf. Romans 6:19) and corruptibility, the merely human in contrast to God and spirit (cf. 3:20; 8:8). Nor is it wise to distinguish a moral sense of 'flesh' which is distinct from that of physical weakness. For Paul, physical weakness is closely tied to moral weakness: it is the weakness of the human condition (that it needs to satisfy its physical appetites) which opens the door to the corruption of these appetites from legitimate desire to illegitimate lust, which in turn opens the door to coveting. It is this all-too-human weakness which undermines the law as God's instrument (8:3). This was also what Paul had in mind when he characterized the human condition as a fatal interaction of humanly weak flesh and passions aroused by sin through the law, in 7:5. We need to remember also that the term 'flesh' enabled Paul to link in the failure of his own people with the general plight of humanity—the fact that they put too much 'confidence in the flesh', not least in 'circumcision in the flesh' (Romans 2:28–29; Galatians 6:13; Philippians 3:3).

Modern translators have shied away from the word 'flesh', presumably thinking it too crude or too old-fashioned. They prefer to translate with paraphrases like 'unspiritual or sinful nature'. But that loses precisely the link which Paul sees to be important in the 'flesh'—the link between human weakness, national pride and sinful lust. Better to regard 'flesh' as one of Paul's technical terms and translate it as such, as 'flesh'.

'I' against 'I'

All too conscious of this fatal weakness of the flesh, Paul expresses the human plight in the most poignant terms. 'I do not know what I do. For that which I commit is not what I want; but what I hate, that I do' (v. 15). The lament is important enough to be repeated (v. 19). At once we see that the 'I' is on both sides of the divide: the 'I' doesn't want to do what it sees to be evil, but the 'I' still does it—the same 'I'. The 'I' wants to do what it knows to be right, but the 'I' fails to do it—the same 'I'. In other words, the 'I' is split. The 'I' has had its consciousness of good and evil informed by the law; but the weakness of the 'I' as flesh means that it succumbs again and again to greed on the one hand, or to apathy on the other.

This analysis thus serves a double function. For one thing, it advances the defence of the law. The willing 'I' acknowledges that the law is good (v. 16). The evil of the 'I's action or inaction is not to be laid at the law's door. But the analysis also does not shift the blame merely to the 'I'. The 'I' is characterized simply as weak—a willing 'I' which lacks sufficient motivation, a fleshly 'I' which lacks the strength to translate will into deed.

The real villain is, once again, sin; Paul makes this point twice also lest it be misunderstood (vv. 17, 20). In so doing, it should be noted, he is looking well beyond the idea of sin as a sequence of sinful acts. He shows that he is conscious of what would now be called corporate or institutional sin—the structures of inheritance and upbringing and society which condition and inhibit the individual and bring about just the frustration that Paul has voiced so honestly here. This is why effective resistance to the power of sin cannot be looked for solely at the level of the individual.

PRAYER

Almighty God, it is when we realize how weak we are,
and how powerful are the forces which corrupt and divert your
good will into looking after ourselves and not stirring our selves
for the sake of others, that we begin to appreciate better
how much we depend on you for all good.

35

ROMANS 7:21–25

The DIVIDED LAW

The law in experience

When we remember that the main object of this chapter is to defend the law from the charge that it is itself sin (7:7), the final thrust of the chapter becomes a little clearer. For Paul here plays with the term 'law' and does so in a rather confusing way. He might even be thought to be describing a sequence of different laws:

- the 'law' which sums up the experience of total frustration just described (v. 21, referring back to 7:14–20)
- the 'law of God' (vv. 22, 25)
- the 'law of sin' (vv. 23, 25).

What are we to make of these different laws?

The second and third should be fairly straightforward. 'The law of God' presumably refers to the law of which Paul speaks in 7:12–13 and 16. It is the law, the Torah, through which God has declared his will for human conduct and for the national life of Israel. The 'I' is able to acknowledge its goodness and to want to follow it.

'The law of sin' likewise refers back to what Paul has been earlier describing. It is the law, the Torah, the same law, but perverted by sin to its own ends. This was just what Paul had been describing in 7:7–13. The law of sin is the law abused by sin. Paul's argument had been designed to bring out the fact that the law should not be blamed for the abuse to which sin puts it.

But note: as with the 'I' in 7:14–20, it is the same law. The law of God is the law of sin, the same law abused by sin. As with the 'I' in 7:14–20, the law is split. As the 'I' succumbs before the power of sin, so does the law. As the 'I' wills to do or not to do and fails, so the law fails to achieve the obedience it calls for. The weakness of the flesh is critical in both cases (7:14, 18; 8:3).

What then of the first 'law'? Some take the first of the three 'laws' in the sense of 'regular pattern', rather like the laws of nature (it is a natural law that summer follows spring follows winter follows autumn). And that makes good sense. But quite possibly Paul wanted to maintain the focus on the law. The law is experienced both as the good law of God and the law of sin. Perhaps Paul tries to pull these different functions of the law together in his talk of another law. Verse 21 thus describes what Paul finds to be the law in experience. What the 'I' actually experiences is the ineffectiveness of the good law abused by sin: it achieves only this frustration of wanting to do good but finding evil the more convenient thing to do. The 'other law' of verse 23 is the reality of the law stretched between announcing God's will and being abused to stir up prohibited passions (7:5). But the precise relation of the three 'laws' is not so important. What is important is to recognize here the self-confusion and anguish which moral sensitivity combined with moral impotence brings about.

The wretched man and his victory

The state of mind just described achieves its most poignant expression in the cry of heartfelt anguish which follows: 'Wretched man am I! Who will deliver me from the body of this death?' (v. 24). It is the anguish of the person caught in the whirlpool of sin: even when caught only in the most outward of the circlings, the pull is unrelenting, and the vortex inescapable; and with it comes the assured extinguishing of life. It is the anguish of one caught in the flypaper of enticement and lust, of self-concern and self-pity, knowing that death comes as the end. It is the anguish of the individual entrapped by social and spiritual forces beyond his or her control and despairing of escape—the body of death.

The difference is that this wretched man knows that escape is possible. And he also knows where that escape is to be found—in 'Jesus Christ our Lord' (v. 25). The gospel, with its message of the power of sin and death broken in the death and resurrection of Christ (6:7–11), provides that answer. It holds out the promise that the law will not always be that frustrating, imprisoning experience. This defence of the law (7:7–24), in other words, does not amount to a complete projection back to the time 'under the law', before grace intervened in Christ (6:14–15). And yet, is this the gospel of redemption already accomplished, or redemption promised? Read on!

PRAYER

Save us, O God, from despair. And when despair threatens, speak to us again of Jesus Christ, of his death and resurrection; minister to us again your grace, revive us in faith, and renew us in hope.

So Then

Who is the 'I'?

Romans chapter 7 has long been a battlefield between commentators unable to agree who it is that Paul had in mind when he spoke of the 'I'. The old view was that Paul was providing biographical information, describing his own spiritual pilgrimage prior to his conversion. On this view the impotent 'I' was Paul convicted of sin, wracked by conscience (over his part in the death of Stephen?) but without any remedy until he was confronted by the living Christ on the road to Damascus. This was a view partly built on the classic conversion stories of Augustine and Luther, both conscience-smitten before they experienced the release of the gospel. The only trouble is that when Paul speaks of his pre-conversion state of mind elsewhere, it is clear enough that he was *not* wracked by conscience (Galatians 1:13–14; Philippians 3:4–6). This view has now generally been abandoned.

It was largely replaced by the view that the 'I' was Everyman—humankind before faith, without faith, outside of Christ, as seen from a Christian perspective. It was not so much Paul's account of what he experienced prior to his conversion, as his post-conversion characterization of his pre-conversion situation. Problematical for this view is the sharpness of the anguish expressed in 7:15–24. This is no mere theorizing: there is real pain and perplexity here. Whoever writes like this is writing from all-too-real and agonizing personal experience.

If 7:7–13 echoes the story of Adam (see Study 33), perhaps it also echoes the history of Israel. For Israel too knew a time 'apart from the law' (7:8; that is, prior to the giving of the law at Mount Sinai); and the coming of the law also saw Israel's fall from grace, in the sin of the golden calf at the foot of the Mount (Exodus 32:1–6). This line of thought could also tie in with the particular sense of 'desire' as sexual desire/lust, for Israel's failure was precisely its fall into idolatry and sexual indulgence (1 Corinthians 10:7–8). In that case, Paul would be recapitulating his earlier indictment (7:5; cf. 1:20–27), but thinking particularly of Israel prior to the coming of Christ (cf. Galatians 3:23–24).

In a case like this we should avoid getting into 'either/or' exegesis.

Most texts are capable of more than one meaning, writers may not themselves have wanted to convey narrowly restricted meanings, and part of the thrill of Bible study is exploring the range of appropriate meaning in a text. But there is a further meaning perhaps worthy of separate consideration.

Christian frustration—and reality

What is striking about the final sentence of chapter 7 is the way it follows not simply the cry of anguish (7:24), but also the cry of triumph (v. 25). By expressing himself in terms of ongoing present tenses, Paul seems to be envisaging an ongoing situation, that is, one which the Christian also continues to share: 'So then, I myself with my mind go on serving the law of God and with my flesh the law of sin' (v. 25). The point, then, is that the Christian does not cease to belong to the generality of humankind by virtue of conversion. The Christian is also the 'I', knowing the anguish and frustration of willing well but still failing badly.

It is quite true that many find such an interpretation very difficult to square with the seriousness of the 'I' described earlier as 'sold under sin' (7:14); 'made prisoner by the law of sin' (7:23). On the other hand, we have already noted that 6:2–11 (particularly 6:5) has to be understood in terms of a process begun but still to be worked through. The placing of 7:25b (after 7:25a) makes the same point. And the point will be reinforced in the next chapter (especially 8:10, 12–13). Christians still have to live in the flesh, and sin is still able to use the law to entice desire into lust. Until death has had its final say, until the process of salvation is completed in resurrection, the split in the 'I' remains. The cry of 7:24 is not so much of despair as of frustration, the frustration of the new life still having to be lived through the old body.

PRAYER

O Lord, the life of the flesh, of self-indulgence in its various forms, is still a feature of my life, even when I deplore it and wish it otherwise. Forgive my continued failure and continue your work of renewal in me until the day of resurrection.

37 ROMANS 8:1–4

The LAW *of the* SPIRIT *of* LIFE

No condemnation

The closing words of chapter 7 may have been realistic, but they may also have been depressing—a victory in prospect ('through Jesus Christ our Lord'), but not yet realized ('So then…'). To redress the balance, therefore, Paul turns again to the confidence in what God has already done in Christ Jesus. The verdict of 'No condemnation' has already been pronounced on those in Christ Jesus (v. 1). Paul will return to just that assurance at the end of the chapter (8:31–34). The process of salvation has begun. It still has a long way to go. The present tension between what has already happened and what has not yet happened causes frustration, at times intense anguish. But the beginning assures the end; the 'already' guarantees the 'not yet'. This is Paul's message in Romans 8.

The key factor is one he has only alluded to thus far in Romans 5 to 8—the Spirit of God (cf. 5:5; 7:6). It is almost as though Paul has been holding back this trump card in order to play it triumphantly in the final round. And that trump card is surely needed. The threat of sin still lingers. Though Christ has conquered its power in his death and new life, those who identify with him have still to experience the full process of death and resurrection worked out in their lives (6:5–11). Moral resolution is required (6:12–19), though the realism of 7:13–25 leaves a clear question as to whether such resolution is sufficient in itself. But the Spirit, the enabling from God to those entrapped by weak flesh, makes a decisive difference. That was what was missing in 7:7–25.

It is not that the Spirit ends human weakness, or somehow short-circuits the often painful process of salvation. Paul will take care to make that clear in what follows. In so doing he will also make clear something that he discovered for himself years earlier (2 Corinthians 12:5–10): it is precisely the way of God to work with and work through human weakness to achieve his ends, since, presumably, there is no other way to work with humankind. Hence the emphasis of 8:18–27 in particular.

The law fulfilled

In this transition passage, Paul completes his defence of the law (7:7—8:4). To the previous variations on the theme—the law of God, the other law, the law of sin (7:22–23)—he adds a further variation, 'the law of the Spirit of life'. He contrasts it with 'the law of sin and death' (v. 2). That at least is already familiar to us: 'the law of sin and death' is the law manipulated by the power of sin to bind humankind closer to death as the only outcome (7:7–13; cf. 5:20; 6:23; 7:5). 'The law of the Spirit of life' is presumably a similar construction, denoting the law now used by the Spirit. In other words, verse 2 is Paul's ultimate expression of the divided law (7:21–23). The law can tragically be used by sin to stir up the covetousness which cripples individuals and their relationships (7:7–11). But the law can also be used by the Spirit to order life in accordance with God's will. The Spirit is the divine counter to the power of sin.

Many find the idea of Paul talking of the law in such a positive way almost impossible to conceive. But it is important to note how verses 1–4 are rounded off. The purpose of God's sending his Son was 'in order that the requirement of the law might be fulfilled in us'. How so? 'In us who walk… in accordance with the Spirit' (v. 4). Paul evidently could speak of 'the law of the Spirit of life' because he saw the law in its life-ordering function as something which those 'led by the Spirit' (8:14) could live by.

What living by the Spirit means in practice, Paul will also elaborate in the following verses. For the moment, however, it is important to register the success of Paul's defence of the law. He has brought it from the point where it seemed no different from sin (7:7). He has shown how sin abused it in enticing desire into lust (7:7–13). He has indicated how the weakness of the fleshly 'I' leaves it incapacitated in temptation (7:14–20). And he has noted the division in the law parallel to that in the 'I' (7:21–23). But now he shows that the law can be the ally of the Spirit, a pointer to the will of God which can be done through the Spirit (vv. 2–4).

PRAYER

Thanks be to God for the Spirit of life, for the Spirit that saves God's law from being a crushing condemnation to being a rule for life, for the Spirit that enables us to live for God. Lord, do not withhold this your Spirit from us.

WHAT GOD HAS DONE *in* CHRIST

Romans 8:3–4 is one of Paul's classic summaries of the gospel. It has everything—God's overall purpose and initiative; the description of the human plight; the person and work of Christ; and the intended outcome in terms of ethical living and the Spirit's enabling.

The human plight

In the order of the Greek in which the sentence was written, it is the human plight which is spoken of first. That plight is summed up on this occasion in terms of the weakness of the flesh and the incapacity of the law to counter it effectively. 'Sin' is not mentioned immediately, but in the light of all that Paul has said in 5:12—8:2 it would have been impossible to avoid mentioning it. Thus in the following clauses it becomes clear again that the real culprit is sin (it is mentioned three times in verse 3). But for the moment it is the fatal combination of a flesh too weak to obey God's law and the law as not fitted to counter that weakness which is in view.

Chapter 8 is where Paul tackles the problem of the flesh. In Romans 6—8 he had set himself to discuss what role (if any) the fearful alliance of sin and death, with the law as their catspaw (5:20), should have in the Christian's life. That interplay of sin and death, and of sin, law and death, in human experience (not excluding that of the believer), has been his main concern in Romans 6—7, though his treatment of them is not yet completed. However, in the course of that exposition it became clear that the flesh and its weakness were a further factor in the equation (7:5, 14, 18). It is that feature on which he initially focuses here.

It is worth recalling that, for Paul, the 'flesh' denotes the fraility of the human being which ends in death, and the weakness of humankind in ever pandering to appetite and desire against humankind's best interest. This is what the law in itself was inadequate to counter; the remedy must come from within.

God's initiative

The subject of the whole sentence is 'God'. Human weakness is such that only God can meet it. He does so in two ways.

First, he sent his Son 'in the very likeness of sinful flesh', that is, to deal with the problem from within. The implication is not that Christ was himself a sinner, but that he shared the flesh of humankind, the flesh whose weakness gave sin its opportunity (7:5). This is Paul's equivalent to Hebrews 4:15. Jesus experienced the fraility of humankind to the full; he knew in personal experience that enticement to personal advantage, for desire to become lust. The real humanity of Jesus was never in question for Paul.

Moreover, he sent Christ also 'for sin'. Since the same phrase is often used in the Greek Old Testament for 'sin offering', that is probably how the phrase here should be translated. Paul again draws on the Old Testament sacrificial system to find the best metaphor for Jesus' death (cf. 3:25). He died as the embodiment of 'sinful flesh'. And thus he (the subject is still 'God') 'condemned sin in the flesh'. In other words, the power of sin had such a hold on human flesh that there was no help for it other than destruction. God is the divine surgeon who recognizes that the cancer of sin has so eaten into the flesh of humanity that there is no salvation for humanity other than by radical surgery, by the complete destruction of that cancerous tissue. That radical surgery took place, as it were, on the cross. The humanity which emerged from the operation is free from the cancer (6:7).

The outcome

The purpose of God's intervention is the rescue and rehabilitation of a humanity which can, after all, live in accordance with God's will (v. 4). So, in addition to sending his Son, God has sent his Spirit. Christ dealt with the weakness of the flesh, and the sin which exploited that weakness, from within the human situation. The Spirit deals with the weakness of the law from within the life of the believer. By countering the power of sin, the power of God counters the power which entrapped the 'I' and thwarted the purpose of God through the law.

PRAYER

Thanks be to God for Christ, who shared our human weakness
all the way to death and experienced the power of sin
in all its enticing attractiveness, but who refused that enticement
and died that we might be free.

39

FLESH *versus* SPIRIT

Before and after coming to faith?

Paul has now set out the alternatives—flesh and Spirit; the weakness of the flesh, the power of the Spirit. In some ways the more expected antithesis would be between sin and Spirit—'the law of sin' and 'the law of the Spirit' (8:2). But Paul seems now to be thinking in terms of human experience from within. In those terms it is the flesh in its weakness and vulnerability to covetousness (7:7–11) which is the main problem. The answer is not the law (8:3), incapacitated as it is in face of that same weakness. The answer is rather the Spirit. Of course, the Spirit is also a power that comes from outside. But Paul in this chapter is thinking of the Spirit primarily as the power which God gives to operate from within the believer (cf. particularly 8:15–16, 23, 26–27). What Paul spells out, then, is the other side of the experience of 7:7–25: the experience of divine enabling, and how that works out in the daily life of the believer.

But first he sets out the two alternatives as starkly as possible—life lived at the level of the flesh as against life lived at the level of the Spirit (v. 5); 'the flesh's way of thinking' as against 'the Spirit's way of thinking' (v. 6). Here again, many commentators tend to become confused. The contrast is so stark—'death' as against 'life and peace' (v. 6). The flesh's way of thinking is hostile to God, cannot submit itself to the law of God (v. 7); those in the flesh are unable to please God (v. 8). In the light of these sentiments, it would seem most natural to assume that Paul is contrasting two groups of people (rather as in 2:7–10). Those of the flesh are the unconverted; those of the Spirit are the believers. On that scenario, the believer has moved from one group to the other (8:9). On this view, 7:7–25 describes life without or prior to faith; 8:1–2, 9 describes the life of faith.

But did Paul see the contrast between the before and after of faith in quite such stark terms? We have already seen cause to doubt that in reference to both chapter 6 and chapter 7; and we shall see further cause to recognize that in Paul the process of salvation is not a once-for-all transition, but a longer drawn-out transition from and through death to life (see particularly 8:23).

The ever-present alternatives

It is more likely, therefore, that Paul uses verses 5–8 to characterize two levels of living. There is a quality of living which is determined by the flesh, and one which is determined by the Spirit. The former 'takes the side of the flesh' (v. 5): the flesh characterizes its mindset (v. 6). That is, when choice is to be made, it opts for what is least inconvenient for itself; how it affects me is always the bottom line. But for Paul, that is the way of death, the way to death (v. 6). It is a mindset which is so turned in upon itself that it can see only short-term and selfish advantage. That is why it is hostile to God and cannot please God (vv. 7–8), for the gracious God always seeks the good of others. And that, by implication, is the alternative Paul sets out—life lived not for the flesh but from the Spirit, a mindset which seeks its goals and its motivation from God. This is the 'lifestyle' Paul hopes to encourage in his readers.

The point is that these two kinds of life are two types of human living, two ideal types, as we might say in the language of social science. That is to say, they do not describe so much actual people—no one is wholly good or wholly bad. Rather they describe the two possibilities which are ever before all human existence. The reality is, on the one hand, the 'split personality' of 7:14–25 and, on the other, the believer into whose life the Spirit has come. Both are caught somewhere on the spectrum which runs between the ideal types: when the Spirit is not brought into account, the anguish of the 'wretched man' of 7:24 is more the norm; when the Spirit is brought into the picture, the fulfilment of God's requirement in the law becomes more a possibility and more an actuality (8:4).

So it is not simply the unbeliever who is vulnerable to the flesh's way of thinking. So long as the believer lives still in the flesh, the body of death, the believer too is vulnerable to that kind of thinking. Believers here are called on not so much to celebrate what God has already done as to recognize the continuing challenge before them.

PRAYER

Grant us, O God, a sober seriousness in the face of our weakness, in face of the powers still set against the accomplishment of your purpose in us, and grant us ever a greater measure of your Spirit to enable us to do what is pleasing to you.

The Spirit Makes the Difference

A Christian defined

At first it would appear that everything just said about 8:5–8 must be mistaken. For Paul seems immediately to affirm (v. 9) that of the two lifestyles set out, his readers have left one behind ('in the flesh') and belong now only and wholly to the other ('in the Spirit'). But that impression will be corrected in verses 10–11. And elsewhere Paul is content to speak of believers as still living 'in the flesh' (Galatians 2:20; Philippians 1:22). It is more likely, then, that Paul is emphasizing the decisive turn which their lives have taken when they accepted the gospel. They have made that fundamental choice, which will determine all future choices, to live for God and not for themselves. In terms of 8:5–8, they have decided for the Spirit as against the flesh. That will not be the end of the story, as 8:12–13 will quickly remind them, just as 6:11–23 will have helped set the more clear-cut metaphors of 6:3–6 in context, and as the painful ambiguity of 7:7–25 will have helped to blunt the sharper imagery of 7:1–6.

It is important to grasp the fact that verse 9 is the nearest thing we have in the New Testament to a definition of a Christian: 'anyone who does not have the Spirit of Christ does not belong to him'. It is the coming of the Spirit which makes the difference—not baptism as such, not even faith as such, but the entry into a receptive life of the power of God. That's what really counts in the shaping of life envisaged in the preceding paragraphs. Also to be noted is the fact that Paul speaks of the Spirit directly. Reception of the Spirit was not simply to be deduced from baptism or confirmation or confession. Rather, the reception of the Spirit was understood as something directly experienced (cf. Acts 19:2), above all in the changed life which it produced. The Spirit experienced in the believer's existence will continue as a theme for several paragraphs.

The Spirit as life

Verses 10–11 provide the immediate balance to verse 9. The continuing reality of the believer's condition is not that death has been left behind. On the contrary, 'the body is (still) dead on account of sin'

(v. 10). This must be the 'body' Paul spoke of in 6:6 ('the body of sin') and in 7:24 ('the body of this death'). In other words, the body of sin (6:6) has not yet been destroyed; the 'I' has not yet been delivered from the body of death (7:24). As verse 10 now makes clear, both these preceding references describe a process whose complete realization still lies in the future. In the present, the believer (the one in whom Christ dwells) still lives through a body destined for death through decay and corruption, a body (flesh) upon which sin can still exercise its enticing power, thus binding it ever more closely to death.

At the same time, however, the presence of the Spirit is the presence of life in the believer. The divine righteousness which re-established the relationship between God and his sinful creation is a counter-thrust to the power of death. The Spirit is the life of God reclaiming the believer for himself. This also means that the process of salvation, the experience of faith, is the experience of both death and life. The believer caught between flesh and Spirit is also caught between death and life. That is what happens when God intervenes in a human life. That intervention does not necessarily bring tranquillity. In fact, it is more likely to bring tension and conflict. It is the life surrendered to the flesh which lacks inner conflict, for the decline through sin to death can be so easy. It is when the Spirit enters a life to contest the sway of sin and counter the weakness of the flesh that conflict ensues. The presence of moral conflict is the sign of the Spirit's presence, not the Spirit's absence.

Verse 11 confirms that the end of the process is the resurrection of the body. Salvation will not be complete until the God who makes alive (4:17) has embraced with life even the body, hitherto given over to death (v. 10). That end is assured, despite the continuing weakness of the flesh and the continuing power of sin, first because it has already been accomplished in Christ, and second because the Spirit who will effect that future resurrection is already active within them. As in 5:1–11, Paul bases his hope both on the gospel of Christ's death and resurrection and on the experience of grace already enjoyed.

PRAYER

Grant that we may know, O God, that experience of life which only your Spirit can give, that life which bubbles up within in praise to you and which shapes all our living more and more towards our sharing in the resurrection of your Son.

41   ROMANS 8:12–17

The SPIRIT SHAPES CHRISTIAN EXPERIENCE

The hesitations which 8:10–11 introduced to the clear-cut antitheses of 8:5–9 are reinforced by verses 12–13. If Paul had been taken to imply that the flesh had been left behind, that death was no longer something to be feared for the Christian, then verses 12–13 should provide sufficient correction. For verses 12–13 call the Christians of Rome, those already directly addressed in 8:9–11, to fresh moral responsibility and endeavour. Paul has to urge these same Christians not 'to live in accordance with the flesh' (the negative lifestyle characterized in 8:5). He has to warn these very same believers that if they so live, 'you will certainly die' (the very state envisaged in 8:6).

It would seem, then, that so far as Paul was concerned, believers as such were not already out of the woods. It was still all too possible for them to live on the level of the flesh, still possible for sin to win the final victory in death. It was precisely the Roman Christians that Paul urged to 'put to death the deeds of the body' (v. 13), that they may live. This double exhortation tell us two things:

- It confirms that salvation, for Paul, was a process not yet complete; that believers were within that process—caught between God's 'already' in Christ's death and resurrection and the gift of the Spirit, and God's 'not yet' because they had still to share fully in Christ's resurrection (8:10–11).

- With this first conclusion comes the all-too-serious warning: it is possible for the believer, even one who already knows the power of the Spirit, to revert to a life lived solely on the level of the flesh, turned away once again from God. Should the Christian so abandon the Spirit, the end will be death. Death is the end of all life lived for itself, whether that of the non-religious or that of the religious.

The Spirit of sonship

Now Paul becomes more reassuring once again. If the Christian can be defined as one who possesses the Spirit of Christ (8:9), so the son of God can be defined in ethical terms as one who is led by the Spirit

(v. 14); that is, as one who seeks inspiration and enabling, not so much in reason or in rule books as in the Spirit within.

This talk of Christians as 'sons of God' (NRSV 'children of God') has several striking features. First, it arises from the believer's identification with Christ. Salvation can now be described as 'adoption' in order to share in Christ's sonship to God (vv. 15–16). Not only Christ's death and resurrection provide a pattern to be repeated in the process of salvation (6:3–11; 7:4; 8:10–11), but now also Christ's sonship. As he is heir of God's inheritance, so Christians will share that inheritance—'heirs of God and joint heirs with Christ' (v. 17). To escape from the talk of life and death into such a different imagery is something of a relief—but not for long.

Again we should note the strongly experiential character of this sonship. It is attested by the Spirit crying 'Abba, Father' (Abba is Aramaic for 'Father'), the very prayer which evidently characterized Jesus' own prayer life (cf. Mark 14:36). And the language used ('cry') implies an experience of some intensity (v. 15). This is the 'witness of the Spirit', which later theologians reduced to something doctrinal and almost rational. But for Paul, the witness of the Spirit was the experience of assurance, whereby early Christians felt and knew the grace of God (v. 16). This was an experience very different from the old one of fear lest the taboos and conventions of their community should be transgressed (v. 15), a fear often expressed in the over-simplifications of fundamentalism. This assurance of the Spirit goes rather with the moral earnestness called for in verses 13–14.

After this sunny interlude, however, the clouds begin to gather again. For the experience of sonship also involves a sharing in his suffering: 'heirs together with Christ, provided that we suffer with him in order that we might also be glorified with him' (v. 17). The pattern of sonship does not displace the pattern of suffering to death and resurrection to glory. Rather, sonship brings a new dimension to the starkness of life and death and helps make the present suffering more bearable while enhancing the hope of future glory.

PRAYER

'Abba, Father,' what a privilege to speak these words. We want to know the witness, Lord, the assurance of your Spirit with our spirits, to strengthen our moral resolution and to sustain us through whatever suffering you appoint for us.

42 ROMANS 8:18–25

The SPIRIT *as the* FIRST INSTALMENT

The groaning of creation

In this passage the full sweep of God's saving purpose becomes clear. It involves a process of suffering, of suffering with Christ (8:17). We are back here with the thought of 5:3–5. There is a beneficial value in suffering: it shapes character (5:4), like gold tested in the fire. But now we touch a deeper level. The suffering in view is necessary in the same way that Christ's suffering and death were necessary. The process of salvation requires humans to go through the same process— but with Christ, and as, in some sense, a sharing in his own suffering and death. The dying of the flesh, the death of death, and the loss of sin's power in death, that is a process of suffering to death indeed; but the Spirit of Christ gives assurance that the sufferings of this phase of the process will be outweighed by the future and final transformation back to the glory once lost (8:17; cf. 1:21; 3:23).

Paul sees the process also in cosmic terms. Indeed he sees it as the final reversal of the failure described in Genesis 3. For according to Genesis 3:17–18, creation itself was caught up in the human failure. Paul here describes it as 'futility' (v. 20), probably thinking of the harshness of agricultural labour, with the many droughts and crop failures, or of the unending cycle of new shoots, growth, withering and decay. Whether he envisaged a glorious, idyllic future, where the ground gives its produce without backbreaking work and in superabundance (a favourite imagining in some circles), we cannot tell. His confidence is simply that a salvation which will liberate the whole of human existence will include also the human environment (vv. 19, 21).

Paul can even sense a sympathetic accord between believers on the way to full salvation and the creation in its out-of-jointedness. Creation is, as it were, in labour, longing to bring to birth the new creation (v. 22). And Christians share that sense of awaiting the consummation, groaning in sympathetic labour as they await the completion of their salvation in the redemption (resurrection) of their bodies. There is scope here for a profound ecological theology. Note that the Spirit is seen as the 'first instalment' of the process, which also brings the guarantee of its completion (v. 23). This also reminds us that, for Paul, the process is not yet complete. Also worth noting is the repetition of the metaphor of 'adoption'. Christians have already received the Spirit of 'adoption' (8:15), but they also await the (completion of the) adoption in the resurrection (v. 23).

Saved in hope

All this gives fuller definition to the hope with which Paul summed up the first major stage of his exposition (5:1–5), where again he integrated it with the thought of suffering—a suffering which did not undercut hope, but which actually strengthened it, again in the light of the experience of the Spirit (5:5; 8:23). The process of suffering, yet to be fully worked through, explains why Paul can speak of salvation in a past, completed tense ('saved'), but only as 'saved in hope'. For hope implies an incomplete process. 'Who hopes for what he (already) sees?' (v. 24). If salvation was complete, then there would be no need for hope: the full fruits of salvation would already be present in experience, and there would be nothing to hope for. But hope is a cardinal Christian virtue precisely because the process of salvation has yet to be worked through in believers' lives; salvation is a goal which still lies in the future (cf. 5:9–10).

At the same time, the phrase ('saved in hope') is not meaningless, precisely because hope for Paul was not something tentative. Hope was rather something assured, based on what had been done in Christ (5:6–10; 8:3, 11) and on what they themselves had already experienced through the Spirit (5:5; 8:2, 9–10, 15–16, 23). So, to use the past tense ('saved') was not inappropriate, so long as the incompleteness of the process was not lost to sight. It is the combination of assurance and hope which makes the waiting a matter of eager longing.

PRAYER

Grant us the sensitivity to be aware when others,
and indeed creation, groan with the labour pains of new life
coming to birth. Help us to share in the hope and anticipation
of this promised birth.

43

ROMANS 8:26–30

HUMAN WEAKNESS & DIVINE PREDESTINATION

When the Spirit prays most effectively

Now comes the climax of Paul's exposition of the Spirit's role in the life and experience of believers, the last mention of the Holy Spirit in the main exposition of the letter (Romans 1—11). This makes what he says all the more striking. He continues with the theme of human weakness; for Paul, the main function of the Spirit in the process of salvation, it would appear, is to counter the weakness of the flesh (v. 26).

This weakness is experienced most frustratingly in prayer. For far from being an effective line of communication between the believer and God, prayer is all too often experienced rather as inability to communicate. The fact is that we do not know what to pray for. It is not so much a question of not knowing how to pray—whether in set forms, or at set times, or anything like that. The problem is rather the complete inability to discern the will of God so that we can, by prayer, align ourselves accordingly. It is the problem of turning to God and then finding ourselves speechless in God's presence.

In this situation the Spirit comes to our aid—not as an intercessor on high, remote from us (cf. 8:34); not with intimations of God's will, so that we can actually pray in meaningful words; not in inspired speech whose beauty or quality clearly demonstrates that it is not of ourselves; but in 'wordless groans'! The climax of Paul's exposition of the work of the Spirit in the believer is not the power of the Spirit nullifying the weakness of the flesh (8:2–4), not the assurance of the Spirit crying 'Abba Father' (8:15–16), not even the groaning in sympathy with the creation (8:23), but the wordless groans of human inability to know what to say before God.

And here is where Paul's description is so astonishing. For the help of the Spirit does not come despite human inarticulateness or to remedy that inarticulateness. The assurance is rather that in and through the believer's own wordless groans the Spirit prays, and prays in tune with God's will (v. 27). It is when believers are most helpless, most tongue-tied, most honest before God in their inadequacy and inability to do more than groan wordlessly, that the Spirit is most active and most effective!

God's assured purpose

The assurance given in this deepest and most embarrassing of human failure (not knowing what to say) is one aspect of a wider confidence in God. The faith which hopes through and in the deepest suffering and frustration is a faith in God as being faithful and reliable in his gracious concern for human flourishing. The believers who can remain confident that the inadequacy of their wordless groans is a mark of their accept-ability to God can also be confident that nothing that happens to them is outside the will of God and that everything works together for their good in fashioning them to be more the people of his calling (v. 28).

The statement which follows is one of the great Bible pronounce-ments about predestination: God's purpose was from the beginning (v. 29), and its completion is assured. Paul can even put all the tenses of verse 30 in the 'past completed' tense: those predestined and called have also been justified and glorified. The purpose of God is so sure. But it is important to remember where this statement comes—not as part of a learned theological discourse on predestination, as a dogma to be rationally defended. The statement here comes at the end of this most profound assertion of how God's Spirit works in and through human weakness to bring assured hope of salvation. The statement regarding predestination arises out of the wonder at what God has already done despite human weakness and through human weakness, out of the recognition that without divine initiative from start to finish there could be no salvation and no hope of salvation. The doctrine of predestination starts as a gasp of wonder.

At the core of the passage is the fitting thought that God seeks to recreate the humanity that failed so badly, into the image of his Son— to beget a new family with Christ as the elder brother (v. 29). But remember: the process includes sharing in his sufferings, and becom-ing like him in his death, in order to attain to the resurrection from the dead with him (Philippians 3:10–11).

PRAYER

Help us in our weakness, Spirit of God; grant us honesty in our
prayers and in our failures in prayer, and shape us through rough
and smooth more and more into the image of Christ.

The TRIUMPH *of* GOD

The final acquittal

In this final, climactic confession of faith and hope, Paul lays aside all hesitation and qualification. His confidence is in God and in the final triumph of God's purpose. Nothing—not human weakness, not demonic power (sin), not death itself—can defeat God or prevent that final triumph. 'If God is for us, who is against us?' (v. 31b). The 'if' does not indicate any doubt on the matter; it could be just as well translated, 'Since God is for us…'. This is the headline which sums up all that follows (vv. 32–39).

The confidence, once again, is rooted in two 'evidences' already familiar to readers (cf. 5:1–11; 8:9–11). First, the reminder of the presence of the Spirit in their lives: 'in view of all these things' (v. 31a) looks back to and includes the whole exposition of life in the Spirit from 8:1–27. And second, the reminder of what God has already done on behalf of his people, in giving his Son to death (v. 32). Very deliberately, Paul echoes one of the most famous episodes in Israel's history—Abraham's offering of Isaac in sacrifice (Genesis 22): 'he did not spare his own son' (v. 32; cf. Genesis 22:16). That total commitment displayed by Abraham in his readiness to sacrifice the one on whom his whole destiny depended (cf. Romans 4:13–21) was a mirror of God's commitment to humankind in the giving of his Son (cf. 8:3).

The assurance needs to include the final judgment. But since the assurance is rooted in what God has already done in Christ, it can remain firm. Christ's death as sin-offering is precisely what provides the assurance that God can be both just and the justifier (3:25–26). When the one who brings about the justification of the ungodly (4:5) is on the judgment throne, then what other charge can be brought against those called by him (v. 33)? When Christ is the advocate on behalf of guilty humankind, then a prosecutor has no chance (v. 34); note also how the familiar confession of Christ's resurrection (cf. 5:10; 6:4, 9–10; 7:4) is supplemented by drawing in Psalm 110:1 (cf. Acts 2:34–35; Hebrews 1:3; 1 Peter 3:22). The justification by faith (5:1) will be fully realized in the final acquittal.

The love of God in Christ Jesus

The confidence in a final, favourable verdict from the judge of all spills over into a final paean of praise for God's protective love in Christ until that consummation of God's triumph. 'Who will separate us from the love of Christ?' (v. 35). The question is rhetorical, expecting either no answer or a negative answer. The list of hardships (v. 35b), no doubt all too real for Paul and many of his readers, is posed simply to be dismissed. The quotation from Psalm 44:22 (v. 36) likewise reflects an experience of persecution already all too real in Paul's missionary work, and soon to be given horrific substance in the persecutions of Christians in Rome by Emperor Nero a few years later. In the face of just such severe persecution, Paul maintains an almost outrageous assurance: 'in all these things we prevail completely, win more than a victory, are more than conquerors through him who loved us' (v. 37). If that had been said by an armchair theologian, it might have been discounted; but the Paul who wrote it wrote also 2 Corinthians 11:23–27. This is no merely pious hope, but confidence in God long tested and proved in experience.

Nothing can quite match the carefully deliberate tone and the wholly sober affirmation of the concluding sentence (vv. 38–39). Nothing, but nothing, can separate from God's love in Christ; the focus on Christ is not to exclude any other expressions of God's love, but to affirm that Christians have found no greater expression of God's love than that displayed through his Son. The list begins, again no doubt deliberately, with the last great enemy, death. The fact that death has still to have its final say in human experience has continued to hang over the treatment of sin, law and death in Romans 6—8 (6:5, 11; 7:24; 8:10–11). Now at last it becomes clear that its power has been exhausted. But neither can life separate from that love—a nice touch for those who find life more threatening than death—and neither can any of the other nameless powers whose baleful influence on human existence is all too evident in human failure, individually and socially. What a confidence! What an assurance!

PRAYER

Speak such words in our ears, O God, every time our resolution begins to slip, and we become depressed by our human weakness and oppressed by the powers ranged against us; and bring us through to share in your triumph.

45 ROMANS 9—11

The PURPOSE of ROMANS 9—11

The function of Romans 9—11 has occasioned a good deal of discussion over the years. Why does Paul suddenly engage in quite a complicated discussion regarding Israel and its future? The words with which he follows the great paean of praise in 8:31–39 seem such an anticlimax. Why this abrupt change in mood and direction? There is a natural tendency for some to regard chapter 8 as the climax to Paul's exposition of the gospel. Is Romans 9—11, then, a kind of afterthought? Perhaps Paul had to hand some sermon or tract he had used on another occasion which he simply added in at this point, before turning, as more commonly in his letters, to consider some ethical implications to his main exposition (chs. 12—15). In view of such questions it is well to consider the purpose of chapters 9—11 as a whole before addressing their argument in detail.

What needs to be grasped right away is that Romans 9—11 is by no means an afterthought. On the contrary, it is better seen as the intended theological climax to the preceding exposition. To see 8:31–39 as the real climax implies that Paul thought of justification and salvation in purely individual terms—the gospel as how the individual's troubled conscience finds peace with God. But to narrow Paul's understanding of the gospel in such a way constitutes a serious misunderstanding of it. Consider the following features of the exposition thus far.

First, Paul's principal theme, the righteousness of God, is a thoroughly Jewish concept. It arises directly from Israel's scriptures (cf. 1:2; 3:2, 19–21; 4:1–25). It is God's commitment to his people, the fulfilment of the obligations he takes upon himself in choosing Israel as his people (see comment on 1:16–17). Paul's principal argument is that precisely this righteousness is now open to Gentile as well as Jew—'Jew first, but also Greek', open to *all* who believe (see Study 4). The unavoidable question arising from that 'all' emphasis is the one now posed: 'What then of Israel? If God's justifying grace is now available to all through faith, then why the choice of Israel in the first place?' It is towards these questions that Paul's exposition has been proceeding.

Second, for Paul, the blessings of the gospel are the blessings for Israel. In particular, we may note how Paul addresses the Roman believers as 'beloved by God, called to be saints', terms drawn directly from Israel's own self-understanding (cf. e.g. Psalms 16:3; 34:9; 60:5; 108:6). The exposition of chapter 4 clearly envisages the uncircumcised inheriting the promises to Abraham equally with the circumcised. Similarly in the final phase of the preceding exposition Paul deliberately invites his readers to think of themselves in terms of Israel's characteristic self-understanding—the saints, those who love God, the called, the firstborn, the elect of God (8:27–30, 33). Here again the question inevitably arises: 'But what does this say about Israel itself?' Paul now attempts to answer that question.

Third, and perhaps most noticeable of all, Paul's indictment of Israel in chapter 2 led to the embarrassing question, 'What advantage then has the Jew?' (3:1). Paul was all too well aware of the serious issue posed—the issue of God's commitment to Israel, the issue of God's faithfulness to his chosen people (3:3–6). Not only Israel's status was in question, but God's very credibility and trustworthiness were at stake. Paul had not been able to deal with the issue then. Chapters 9—11 are where he tackles it. In a real sense the whole of what has gone before has been building up to this most fundamental of theological questions, the question of what God is about.

It is also important, therefore, to see that the subject of chapters 9—11 is Israel and God's purpose for Israel. Many regard that subject as Israel and the Church, often with the implication that the Church has somehow replaced Israel in God's love and superseded Israel in God's purpose. But it can quickly be seen that the subject of Romans 9—11 from start to finish is Israel and only Israel. The lament of the opening verses is over Israel (9:1–5). The issue to be dealt with in chapters 9—11 is posed in 9:6: the issue of how Israel should understand itself and whether God's word regarding Israel and to Israel has failed. And that issue comes to successful resolution in the conclusion of 11:26 and 28. Fittingly, the exposition is rounded off with a doxology to the one God, celebrating the depth of his riches and the incomprehensibility of his ways (11:33–36).

PRAYER

Lift up our eyes, O God, to recognize that you are concerned with nations and peoples as well as individuals, and keep us from trivializing thought of your purposes by narrowing them to the limitations of our comprehension.

46

WHAT HAS HAPPENED *to* ISRAEL?

Paul's anguish for his people

Perhaps we should assume that Paul broke off his dictation of Romans at the end of 8:39, and only resumed it after a break, or next day. But as it now reads, the letter itself plucks us from the heights of 8:31–39 and plunges us into the depths of 9:1–3, from an elect of God that inspires Paul's fullest confidence (8:33) to an elect of God that brings him nearly to despair (9:2–3). And this is no casual turn. Paul's oath of honesty in verse 1, with his triple affirmation, is among the most solemn utterances he ever penned. His grief was great and the anguish of his heart unceasing (v. 2). This is not someone who has abandoned his own people and now cares nothing for them. Of course there will be some rhetorical emphasis, even exaggeration here, but Paul clearly wants to be believed and believes that what follows is of utmost importance for his people.

In verse 3 Paul deliberately echoes the prayer of Moses in Exodus 32:32, where Moses interceded for Israel following the apostasy of the golden calf: 'But now, if you will only forgive their sin—but if not, blot me out of the book that you have written.' Paul in turn expresses his willingness to be accursed, cut off from Christ, for the sake of his kinsfolk. Nothing is said at this point about the reason for his anguish and willingness for self-sacrificing martyrdom. The implication is clear, not least in the light of the parallel with Exodus 32, that Israel has somehow failed. But Paul evidently wanted to unveil the full scope of his exposition only gradually. Rather as he had in Romans 2, where the identity of the one being criticized only became clear little by little as the 'Jew' of 2:17, so here Paul finds it necessary to unfold the plight of Israel, the character of Israel, and Israel's role within the purpose of God little by little.

The blessings of Israel

Paul starts by reminding his readers of Israel's advantages (cf. 3:1). He starts by affirming that his kinsfolk *are* Israelites' (v. 4). The tense is important—not that they were Israelites or had ceased to be Israelites. They still retained the special position before God of being the descendants of the patriarchs to whom the promises had been given; their calling to be Israel had not been revoked.

The listing of Israel's continuing blessings has a familiar ring. For these were precisely the blessings in which Christians were now rejoicing—'adoption' (cf. 8:15, 23), 'glory' (cf. 5:2; 8:18, 21), 'the covenants' (cf. the familiar words used in connection with the Lord's Supper, 1 Corinthians 11:25). 'The giving of the law' certainly characterized Israel's own focus on the law, but Paul had also tried to claim that in some sense as a blessing for those of faith and the Spirit (3:31; 8:4). 'The service' had in mind the worship of the Jerusalem Temple, but Paul thought of his own 'service' (in the gospel) in just the same terms (1:9; 15:16). 'The promises' of course evoked again God's promises to the fathers, but here too Paul had gone out of his way in 4:13–21 to argue that the promise to Abraham had the uncircumcised also in view. And even 'the fathers' Paul had felt free to claim for the 'us' on whose behalf he wrote (4:1). Paul, in other words, does not duck the challenge his exposition of the gospel throws up: how can these blessings be both the blessings of Israel and the blessings of 'all who believe', Gentile as well as Jew?

The final item on the list begins to provide something of the answer. For the chief of Israel's blessings is the Messiah born of Israel's stock. The implication hinted at, but yet to be expounded, is that the vital clue to the conundrum lies in Israel's own Messiah (v. 5).

The closing doxology unfortunately has distracted attention from that implication, since it is usually taken as a doxology to Christ as 'God' ('the Messiah who is over all, God…', NRSV). But Paul's thought is dominated more by his sense that Israel's Messiah has a central place within the climax of God's purpose. As when he has celebrated the mystery of that purpose in 11:25–32 he exclaims in wonder at the God who so orders things (11:32–36), so here the thought of Israel's Christ probably drew from him a similar exclamation in blessing of this 'God who is over all'.

PRAYER

Blessed are you, O God, who has called your people Israel,
has blessed them so richly, and has given us also share in these
blessings through the one you sent to Israel as your Messiah.
Blessed are you, one God, over all.

WHO IS ISRAEL?

Has God's word failed?

Verse 6 sets the agenda. Despite appearances (by implication, Israel's large-scale rejection of its Messiah), God's word has not failed. That word will certainly include God's promises to Israel and purpose for Israel, as alluded to in 9:4–5. It is their evident failure to be realized (from a Christian perspective) which poses the issue. What pained Paul so deeply was Israel's implied refusal of the gospel. If Israel had refused the one whom Christians hailed as Israel's own Messiah, then what did that mean? Not, surely, that God's word and will had been blocked: if Paul was confident of anything, it was the surety of God's accomplishing his purpose. The answer must rather lie with Israel itself. Hence the focus on Israel as Paul attempts to answer the questions posed by Israel's unbelief.

Also to be noted is the extent to which Paul uses scripture in the following chapters (more intensively than in anything else he wrote), and the extent to which his argument in defence of this opening affirmation depends on scripture. We will try to document this sufficiently in what follows. Paul rebuts the suggestion that God's word, God's purpose as indicated through scripture, has failed; on the contrary, scripture provides a clearer indication of God's purpose than has usually been realized.

Defining Israel

Paul's opening statement again provides both a headline and a key to unlock what follows. However, its very epigrammatic terseness has left its meaning unclear—literally, 'All those from Israel, these are not Israel', or slightly elaborated, 'Not all those descended from Israel are Israel'. What does Paul mean?

Paul seems to have two Israels in mind. One is national or ethnic Israel, that is, those who are from the patriarchs by physical line of descent. That seems clear enough from what follows. But the other? The usual answer is the Church, made up of believing Jews and Gentiles. The implication, then, is that the title 'Israel' has passed from ethnic Israel to the Church: the Church is actually the 'real'

Israel of God's purpose. That reading has attracted many commentators over the centuries. But, as already suggested in Study 45, that reading should probably be regarded as a misreading. As the olive tree allegory confirms later (11:17–24), there is only one Israel in view (one tree, not two, and not another tree replacing the original tree).

The real contrast posed in verse 6 is not between two Israels, but between Israel and not-Israel. The real question is, 'Who is Israel? What constitutes Israel as Israel?' Paul's immediate answer is clear and comes in two parts. First (vv. 7–9), 'Israel' is not defined in terms of physical descent; otherwise Ishmael (Abraham's child through Hagar) would have as much right to be designated 'Israel' as Isaac. But the line of Abraham's seed which constitutes 'Israel' comes not just through physical descent, it also comes through promise; it is in and through Isaac alone that the promised seed is given, the promised seed which constitutes Israel. Paul here will have been thinking of the account already heavily drawn upon in chapter 4.

Second (vv. 10–13), the identity of 'Israel' is not determined by what people (Jews) do, by works (of the law); otherwise Esau might have had a higher claim to this sonship than Jacob. The allusion, of course, is to the accounts in Genesis 25 and 27 (it is 25:23 which is cited in verse 12). More disputed is what Paul had in mind in the criteria of identity which he dismissed. 'Anything good or bad' (v. 11) is left vague, to cover every kind of human activity, presumably with the later lifestyles of Esau and Jacob particularly in mind. 'Not of works' (v. 12) echoes, no doubt deliberately, the formula used in 3:20 and 4:2, later picked up again in 9:32: in other words, what is in view are the actions done in obedience to the law which Jews usually saw as setting them apart from the other nations. In contrast (vv. 11–12), what really constituted Israel's identity was the election ('the purpose of God in terms of his free choice') and the call of God ('call' is the main linking word in this section: 9:7, 11, 24–26). Not what *Israel* does constitutes Israel, but what *God* has done.

PRAYER

Your word holds immeasurable treasures for us.
But we so easily misunderstand it, and even corrupt its meaning
for our own advantage. Teach us how to read, understand
and observe it aright.

GOD'S PURPOSE *in* ISRAEL'S HISTORY

The final verse of the previous paragraph, 9:13, as elsewhere in Paul, provides both the conclusion to the preceding argument and also the heading for what follows: 'Jacob I have loved, but Esau I have hated'. The quotation is from Malachi 1:2–3; and most of those listening to Paul's letter being read out in the Roman house churches would have been well enough aware that in speaking of 'Jacob', 'Israel' was in mind, 'Israel' being God's new name for Jacob (Genesis 32:27).

'Jacob I have loved'

Paul was well aware of the unsavoury implications of the Malachi 1:2–3 quotation. If God 'hated' Esau, prior to and without regard for anything Esau was later to do (9:11–12), then that puts a serious question mark against any thought of God being just (v. 14). It is to Paul's credit that he does not ignore or duck this issue but poses it squarely. At the same time we need to recall that the force of his argument is only revealing itself slowly. As we shall see, it is in the interest of his larger argument that Paul sets out this issue so sharply. But here we should note again that the question of Israel unavoidably involves the question of God. The crisis of Israel and the gospel is also a crisis of God: as in 2:24, it is God's name (the very credibility of theism) which is at stake in all this.

Paul's first response is to cite one of Israel's most famous credal assertions about God: 'I will have mercy on whom I have mercy, and I will show compassion to whom I show compassion' (v. 15). The quotation is directly from Exodus 33:19, God's self-revelation to Moses. This is an initial statement of the even more famous and influential Exodus 34:6–7: 'The Lord, the Lord, a God merciful and gracious, slow to anger, and abounding in steadfast love and faithfulness', itself a basic staple in Israel's confession of God (e.g. Numbers 14:18; Nehemiah 9:17; Psalm 86:15; 103:8; 145:8; Joel 2:13; Jonah 4:2). Prior to God's revelation in Christ, this, we might say, was the fullest, most intimate self-revelation of God.

The point of greatest significance is that this self-revelation was in terms of 'mercy', as Paul is quick to point out (v. 16). If there is any word which foreshadows the conclusion towards which Paul is striving in this exposition, it is this word 'mercy' (9:15–18, 23; 11:30–32). The central feature of God's character, the feature which determines his purpose, the feature on which Paul relies in denying the question of verse 14, is God's mercy. On that rock he rests, and here his bemused questionings of the twists and turns in the working out of God's purpose find their answer.

'Esau have I hated'

Paul does not forget the other half of Malachi 1:2–3, for it also is important in his overall exposition regarding Israel. As Moses' experience of God elaborated the thoughts of God's care for Israel, so God's word to Pharaoh elaborated the word regarding Esau (v. 17). The quotation in this case is from Exodus 9:16. To be noted is the fact that Pharaoh is presented as a foil to God's saving actions on behalf of Israel; that was why Pharaoh was raised up, so that the account of God's rescue of Israel from Pharaoh's power might spread abroad his reputation. This is the uncomfortable, disquieting implication of God's mercy to one person, that it is displayed at cost to others.

Paul again refuses to shirk the implication: 'So then to whom he will he shows mercy, but whom he wills he hardens' (v. 18). The last verb ('harden') is a deliberate echo of the term used several times in the Exodus narrative. At times it could be interpreted as a self-hardening on the part of Pharaoh (Exodus 7:22; 8:15; 9:35; 13:15); but Paul does not duck the obvious implication elsewhere (e.g. Exodus 4:21; 7:3; 9:12; 10:1) that such hardening is (also) the work of God.

To be noted again is that Paul is here playing to the gallery; this is Israel's reading of its own history. In celebrating God's goodness to one people, it is easy to dismiss the fact that other peoples have suffered as a result. But Paul takes this tack because he is preparing to turn the tables on this Israel which exults in the mercy shown to itself and is relatively unmoved by the hardening of others which made its own triumph possible.

PRAYER

God of mercy, what is this mercy which entails the hatred and hardening of others? Permit us never to rest content in our experience of your goodness to us without asking disquieting questions regarding how others have fared in consequence.

The PROBLEM of PREDESTINATION

The potter and the clay

Once again Paul faces up to the problem his exposition has posed: if God hardens, if he determines a Pharaoh's refusal, how can he hold Pharaoh responsible for that refusal (v. 19)? The problem, of course, is not simply religious. If individuals are predetermined by their inherited genes, and/or by the social context in which they are brought up and educated, are the decisions they make genuinely free decisions, or simply the interplay of chemicals and electric impulses in their brains, simply the intersection of social forces over which they have no control? Nevertheless, Israel's history poses the issue in its sharpest form as the relationship of God's predestination and providence with human free will and responsibility.

The initial response seems brutally cold and harsh. Paul reverts to the ancient image of God as potter (vv. 20–21). Verse 20 echoes Isaiah 29:16 ('Does the thing made say to its maker?') and Isaiah 45:9 ('Why have you made me thus?'). The thought, of course, is of God as Creator. And however much the human sense of its own dignity rebels against the thought, preferring to see ourselves as gods, and creators in our own right (cf. Genesis 3:5), it is important for humans to acknowledge the infinite qualitative distinction between Creator and creation, the gap between substance made and shaped on the one hand, and the mind and power which creates on the other—however much other images (e.g. of birth and family) are called upon as well. In taking properly into account that infinite difference, it is quite right to express the relative insignificance of the creature in terms of the impossibility of even imagining the thing made answering back to the maker, 'Why have you made me thus?'

Paul will have been well aware of the famous imagery of the potter in Jeremiah 18:1–11 and presumably wished his readership to recall it also. The point is that, more clearly there than in any other of the potter-and-clay passages in the Old Testament, it is Israel itself who is being addressed. What is also noticeable is that the passage is intended as a warning to Israel—a warning intended, interestingly, to recall Israel to repentance. In other words, the passage recalled here had no difficulty in squaring thought of God as potter with thought of Israel's responsibility before God. Instead of using the harshness of the potter image to explain God's harshness to the Esaus and Pharaohs of the world, it is the puzzle of Israel's own behaviour and the implied harshness of God to *Israel* itself which needs to be taken into account.

Objects of wrath and objects of mercy

The formulation of verses 22–23 leaves the problem open: 'what if...?' Paul does not yet claim to see the full sweep of God's purpose. He recognizes the logic of the potter imagery: there are pots made for demeaning use, and there are pots (elegant vases) shaped for glorious use. In both cases the generosity of God is manifest—in the one case, his patience; in the other, his mercy (that key word again). All this is fully borne out by history. The fact that there are individuals and even peoples who seem to be set and to set themselves on the downward road to destruction is a repeated lesson of history. Likewise, the confident hope of those with faith is always held in recognition that, in all this, they are the products of God's mercy. As noted before (Study 43), belief in predestination grows directly from the creature's humble sense that everything good and hoped for has come from and is wholly dependent on God alone.

Once again, however, the subversive note in Paul's exposition should not be missed. Paul is not simply appealing to a bald theology of predestination on his own account. He is referring to the only theology of predestination he actually knew—Israel's sense of its election as God's chosen 'objects of mercy', with the Esaus and the Pharaohs cast in the negative supporting role. But it is just that theology of predestination which Paul has been arguing against. Perhaps it is the fuller theology of predestination (including the negative implication of 'objects of wrath') to which Israel has to refer if it is to understand its present situation. Israel are the objects of mercy; but who is Israel?

PRAYER

Lord, our pride rebels against the thought of being mere clay pots, shaped entirely to serve your larger purpose. Grant us a proper sense of humility, and an appropriate sense of responsibility before you for what we are.

THOSE WHOM GOD HAS CALLED

Both Jews and Gentiles

Only now does Paul's subversive strategy begin to emerge to the surface. For everything said so far about God's calling and about God's predetermining of destinies has been in terms drawn directly from Israel's scriptures, and has had Israel's own history directly in view. It is Isaac, Jacob and Israel who were the chosen ones and Ishmael, Esau and Pharaoh who were destined for the negative complementary roles. So the faithful Jew could well have read 9:1–23 with the unshadowed assumption that his people, ethnic Israel, were the 'objects of mercy prepared beforehand for glory' (9:23). In fact, however, Paul has been preparing to turn the tables—first, by redefining Israel, or rather by recalling Israel to what really constituted its identity as Israel (9:6–13); and second, by reminding them that the calling of this Israel has the less savoury consequence of the rejection of not-Israel. What Paul sets in hand at verse 24 is to indicate to his readers who now fits this definition of Israel (9:24—10:17), and what role ethnic Israel itself now fills within the divine plan (10:18—11:32).

Who, then, are 'the objects of mercy'? Paul replies, 'Those whom God has called, us, not only from Jews but also from Gentiles' (v. 24). If 'Israel' is to be defined in terms of God's call (9:7–12), then the fact for Paul is that the 'called' of God now include Gentiles as well as Jews (1:6–7; 8:28, 30). This is one of only two times in chapters 9—11 (the other is 10:12) that Paul recalls the Jew/Gentile (Greek) antithesis which featured so strongly in the earlier section of his exposition (1:16; 2:9–10; 3:9). In chapters 9—11 he has replaced that dichotomy with the single term 'Israel'. The point is that the 'Jew/Gentile' divide is left behind when the thought turns to Israel: Israel, properly understood, transcends and absorbs that old distinction.

Paul develops the point (vv. 25–26) by citing two passages from Hosea (2:23 and 1:10). Both celebrate God's amazing grace in choosing and sustaining Israel, mirrored in the fantastic tolerance and faithfulness of Hosea to his adulterous wife. The point is the language used in both passages. God's election amounted to the choice of 'not my people' to be God's people, to be 'sons of the living God'. This is what it means to be Israel—the transformation of not-Israel to become Israel, 'not my people' to become God's chosen ones. This was Hosea's own perception of what it meant to be God's people. And it is this definition of Israel which is now most clearly fulfilled by Gentiles, the not-Israel become Israel by God's call.

But including the remnant of Israel

The overturning of Israel's old self-understanding does not mean a total abandonment of that self-understanding. It is not that Gentiles have replaced Jews in Israel-defined-by-God's-call. Rather, Israel properly defined includes both—and that means and includes ethnic Israel. For Hosea had also spoken in the same context of 'the sons of Israel' numbered 'like the sand of the sea' (Hosea 1:10; itself an echo of the promise to Jacob about to become Israel, Genesis 32:12). And Isaiah took up precisely the same imagery in predicting that of this innumerable Israel, 'only a remnant of them will be saved', a purpose which God would complete and cut short in performing his word on the earth (vv. 27–28; Isaiah 10:22–23).

The earlier passage in Isaiah's prophecy had similarly anticipated a drastic reduction of Israel's seed (v. 29; Isaiah 1:9). To be noted is the use of the important word 'seed', a major link back to the earlier exposition in 4:13–18; also that the parallels cited (Sodom and Gomorrah) are known in biblical history as destroyed by divine judgment (Genesis 18:16—19:29; Isaiah 13:19; Amos 4:11). Here again Paul is hinting (as had Isaiah) that the unfavoured figures in Israel's history of divine election (Esau, Pharaoh, and now Sodom and Gomorrah) provide a warning for Israel itself.

The theme of Israel being reduced to a 'remnant' is well established in Israel's scriptures, both as a warning and a reassurance (e.g. 2 Kings 19:31; 21:14; Ezekiel 5:10; Micah 5:7–8). Both aspects are appropriate here and call into further serious question any presumption that Israel is to be identified straightforwardly with ethnic Israel. The Israel to be saved in the end might well be a much smaller group.

PRAYER

Mysterious God, in your right hand is mercy, in your left hand judgment. We cannot see how you hold them in balance. Grant us, while relying on the one, a proper fear of the other.

ISRAEL'S STUMBLING

Pursuing the law of righteousness

Paul sums up to where his exposition has reached—'What then shall we say?' (v. 30). The summary brings to focus all that he has been saying about Gentiles and Israel, not only in chapter 9 but also in the earlier argument. The key word is once again 'righteousness' (four times in vv. 30–31), recalling its crucial role in 1:17, 3:5, 21–26 and 4:3–22. In each case, it will be recalled, it is the word which sums up Israel's perception of the obligation which God took upon himself in making covenant with Israel. God is righteous when he fulfils the promises he made to the fathers, when he saves and sustains Israel. Israel is righteous when it fulfils its obligation to live as God's people.

The amazing feature of the gospel's success, however, is what it has meant in terms of righteousness for the Gentiles. Gentiles were outside that covenant (between God and Israel); they therefore did not pursue that relationship or seek to live accordingly. Nevertheless, the realization that what God wants first and foremost from humankind is trust in him has meant that believing Gentiles have, in fact, 'attained... the righteousness which is from faith' (v. 30).

In contrast, Israel with whom the covenant had been made (the covenant which defined righteousness) had missed the mark. At this point Paul's language is worthy of note. For while he speaks of Gentiles 'not pursuing righteousness' but nevertheless 'attaining righteousness', he speaks of Israel 'pursuing the law of righteousness', but 'not reaching the law' (v. 31; some translations find the language so puzzling that they change it). Here, in other words, Paul again recognizes the positive function of the law—that is, presumably, the law as defining righteousness. To 'reach the law' (v. 31) is evidently the same as 'attaining righteousness' (v. 30).

So what makes the difference? Wherein does Israel's failure lie? What is it that Gentiles have 'attained' but Israel failed to 'reach'? Verse 32 provides the explanation. Israel failed because they understood and attempted to fulfil the law in terms of 'works' (referring back to 3:20, 27–28; 4:2). They thought that righteousness meant maintaining the practices of the law by which they could boast of their status over other nations (2:17–23; 3:10–18), 'works' as reinforcing the conviction that God was in effect God only of Jews (3:27–29). They had not appreciated that the law pointed first and foremost to the need for trust in the one God, that God's will (law) is fulfilled by those who live out of faith in God (3:27, 31).

The stumbling stone of Christ

It was the gospel of Christ which had brought this home to Gentile believers. Unhappily for Israel, the proclamation of Christ had proved to be a 'stone of stumbling' (v. 32), an obstacle over which they had tripped—Paul retains the metaphor of a race or pursuit by using a familiar image (Exodus 23:33; Ecclesiasticus 31:7). That Christ is in view is not clear on the surface of the exposition; Paul continues to unveil the full thrust of his argument only slowly.

The quotation which follows (v. 33) is a mixture of Isaiah 28:16 ('Behold I am laying in Zion a stone... he who believes in him will not be ashamed') and Isaiah 8:14 ('...a stone of offence and a rock of stumbling'). It is uncertain whether Isaiah 28:16 was already interpreted as a reference to Messiah in Jewish circles. But it is clear that it was so interpreted early on by Christians (1 Peter 2:6–8). In conjunction with Psalm 118:22 (Mark 12:10–11; Acts 4:11), this sequence of 'stone' references provided a powerful imagery both for the reversal which the first Christians saw in Christ's death and resurrection, and also as an explanation of why Israel had rejected its Messiah—the stone rejected by the builders has become the chief cornerstone.

In terms of Paul's exposition, the Messiah who had actually come did not fit Israel's expectations, as measured by the law understood in terms of works; he became an obstacle to them. But in fact Jesus' death and resurrection provide the major focus for faith, the same faith as that exercised by Abraham (Romans 4), a faith which would be a source of firm confidence and of no embarrassment (cf. 1:16).

PRAYER

Christ, you are the stone rejected, the stumbling stone, become the chief cornerstone. In our pursuit of righteousness, ever bring us to renewed and deeper faith, and let us never be ashamed.

CHRIST IS *the* END *of the* LAW

Establishing righteousness as their own

The chapter break between Romans 9 and 10 is unfortunate, since the section 9:30—10:4 is a paragraph of unbroken exposition. The contrast between a righteousness open to Gentiles and a righteousness misunderstood by Israel continues through to 10:4. Paul's expression of concern for his own people (v. 1) may sound like a fresh beginning, rather like 9:1–2 and 11:1, but it is provoked by the frustration expressed (9:31–33); and the critique of Israel continues without a break in 10:2–3, using the same terms, and probably retaining the imagery of the race in 10:4. Paul was evidently concerned lest his critique of Israel be understood as a rejection of Israel. On the contrary, his longing for their salvation remained unabated, and all the more pressing as a result of their present 'stumbling' (v. 1).

Paul readily acknowledges Israel's religious dedication; he makes solemn affirmation of it. The only trouble in his view is that it has been misdirected: 'They have a zeal for God—but not in accordance with knowledge' (v. 2). Here Paul was almost certainly thinking of Israel's tradition of sacred 'zeal'. The heroes of zeal had been much celebrated—particularly Phinehas (Numbers 25:10–13), Elijah (1 Kings 18:20–40) and Mattathias, first leader of the revolt against the Syrians—in Ecclesiasticus 45:23–24; 48:2 and 1 Maccabees 2:24–28, 54, 58. Paul himself had been such a 'zealot' (Galatians 1:13–14), as expressed particularly in his persecution of the church (Philippians 3:6). The point was that this 'zeal' was directed mainly to the preservation of Israel's purity from contamination by other peoples and their practices, and also that it had expressed itself in violence against Israelites/Jews as well as foreigners—whoever had threatened Israel's sacred set-apartness to God. It is presumably this isolationism which Paul had particularly in mind when he castigated Israel's zeal as lacking in knowledge.

Israel had misunderstood God's righteousness (in the way just indicated in 9:32) and 'sought to establish their own' (v. 3). The criticism is usually taken to mean the attempt to achieve righteousness by their own efforts. But 'their own' here normally has the sense of 'their own' as peculiar to them, belonging to them and not to others. In other words, we are back with the religiosity of 2:17–23 and 3:27–29. Israel's mistake was to regard righteousness not as the result of God's call received in faith, but as something which belonged to Israel alone. It was this understanding of Israel's covenant and law as designed to keep Gentiles out which Paul most objected to as a misunderstanding and indeed perversion of God's covenant grace and righteousness.

Righteousness for all who believe

If we have understood the thrust of verses 1–3 (9:30—10:3) aright, then verse 4 should probably fall into place. Here again, traditional exposition has usually taken verse 4 to speak of 'Christ as the end of the law'. The implication drawn is that Christ, by his death and resurrection, brought an end to the law, and left it with no role in the process of salvation. However, that interpretation does not seem to take enough account of the positive role still attributed by Paul to the law in passages like 2:12–16; 3:31 and 8:2–4. Others take 'end' in the quite proper sense of 'goal', understanding Paul as continuing the race metaphor started in 9:30: Christ is the goal of the law. This may be part of Paul's meaning, though 'goal' achieved would normally imply race ended, and there is still the negative critique of 9:32 and 10:2–3 to be taken into account.

Probably, therefore, Paul meant that Christ marked the end for the false understanding of the law implied in these verses (9:31–32; 10:2–3). Christ's mission (9:33) reasserted the fact that God's righteousness is given to faith, that God only draws to himself the humbly trustful and (can) only sustain them as they continue in that faith. Once again, righteousness is for all who believe.

PRAYER

O God, we are always tempted to clutch your grace to ourselves as something peculiarly ours, as though the thought that your grace is for all is something threatening to us. Forgive us our narrow-mindedness, and ever challenge us afresh with the realization that faith and grace far transcend all our narrow horizons.

The TWO KINDS *of* RIGHTEOUSNESS

Paul continues the contrast between the two understandings of right-eousness which he began to expound in 9:30–32 and continued in 10:3. He characterizes the difference now as difference between two kinds of righteousness—'the righteousness which is from the law' (v. 5), and 'the righteousness from faith' (v. 6).

The righteousness from the law

By this 'righteousness' Paul presumably means the mistaken under-standing of Israel criticized in 9:32 and 10:2–3. As we have seen, that misunderstanding has traditionally been taken to be the mistaken belief that righteousness was to be earned by obedience to the law, by doing good works. That interpretation in turn is usually taken to be supported by the text cited: 'He who does these things will live in them'. The text is from Leviticus 18:5, usually understood to promise life (life in the world to come, eternal life) on the basis of obeying the law. On this basis, 'the righteousness from the law' is typically inter-preted as stigmatizing Israel's belief that they had to obey the law in order to win God's favour and assure their place in the world to come.

However, we have already noted that Israel's failure was conceived by Paul in rather different terms (9:30–32; 10:2–3). And in fact the force of Leviticus 18:5 seems to be rather different also. What Levit-icus 18:5 spelled out was indeed what might be described as the terms of the covenant made by God with Israel. But what these terms actually amounted to was that obedience was to be the way of life. Leviticus 18:5 in effect says, 'Here is how you must live within my covenant and as my covenant people; you shall live by doing them.' What is envisaged is a way of life which will be maintained and extended by following these rules—long life. This was also the way Leviticus 18:5 was understood in one of its earliest commentaries, Ezekiel 20:5–26 (note the references in 20:11, 13, 21): by doing these things, life would be regulated and lived out as God's people; without them it was impossible to live the life of the covenant people (Ezekiel 20:25).

So 'the righteousness of the law' is conceived as the life of Israel regulated by the law. The only problem was that by focusing so much on the law as regulating Israel's life, its wider application was lost to sight, and the more fundamental role of faith in the divine/human relationship likewise (cf. Galatians 3:12).

The righteousness from faith

In contrast, 'the righteousness from faith' is better characterized by another scripture, Deuteronomy 30:12–14. To be noted at once is the fact that Deuteronomy 30:12–14 speaks also of the law. Deuteronomy 30:12–14 was itself an exhortation to 'choose life' (30:15, 19). The offer held out to Israel was precisely the same as that summarized in Leviticus 18:5: by obeying these comandments you will live long in the land and enjoy length of days (Deuteronomy 30:16–20). The exhortation of Deuteronomy 30:12–14 is actually to emphasize how easy it is to keep the law: it is not far from you, but near, 'in your mouth and in your heart so that you can do it' (Deuteronomy 30:14). That is to say, once again Paul is not simply contrasting law with faith. Rather, he is elaborating the contrast of law understood simply as marking out Israel's distinctive way of life, with the law understood as of more general application.

It is this latter point which Paul brings out in his line-by-line exposition of Deuteronomy 30:12–14 (vv. 6–8). In this he was no doubt greatly helped by the fact that other Jewish expositors had already seen Deuteronomy 30:12–14 as of wider relevance. The law was in fact the embodiment of a higher, more universal expression of God's wisdom (cf. Baruch 3:29—4:1). The somewhat mysterious language of Deuteronomy 30:12–14 indicated that God's will for human flourishing has a deeper source than Israel's law and a more universal outreach than Israel. That higher/deeper character is now most clearly expressed in Christ, in his ascension and in his resurrection. So as Deuteronomy points beyond the law to the universal wisdom of God, so the word on lip and in heart can be seen as pointing beyond to the fuller revelation of the gospel.

PRAYER

Once again we ask of you, O God, that you will enable us to discern the difference between blind obedience and faithful trust in you, and to live out the difference in our living.

SALVATION *for* ALL

Faith and confession

Paul has made the bold identification of 'the word which is near' with 'the word of faith which we proclaim' (10:8). It is not the case, we need to stress again, that he sees 'the word of faith' as utterly opposed to the law or as wholly displacing the law. Rather we need to recognize that Paul saw the law as pointing beyond itself to that more fundamental relationship with God, dependent on faith. It is this more fundamental relationship which he sees most clearly and fully expressed now in the gospel. The gospel, on lip and heart, now speaks more universally than the law on lip and heart had ever reached (10:8). This is precisely the gospel which proclaims Jesus' resurrection and exaltation (10:6–7).

Paul refers in verse 9 almost certainly to one of the earliest Christian confessions. And since the talk is of belief and confession, it is likely that Paul had in mind a very early form of baptismal confession, perhaps the earliest. In deciding to respond to the gospel, the would-be Christian took a double step, the order here (confession and belief) being determined by the order of phrases in Deuteronomy 30:14 (on lip and in heart). He believed 'in his heart' (the verb denotes an act of belief) that 'God had raised him from the dead' (one of the most regular early confessional forms; see comment on 4:24). But belief in the heart was not sufficient in itself. Confession 'with the mouth' was also vital (v. 10). If baptism was indeed in mind, then Paul was no doubt envisaging the vital importance of a public stand being taken, of a public confession which might have serious family and social consequences for the person being baptized. But nothing short of that would do. The public nature of the commitment was the measure of the seriousness of the commitment.

It is noteworthy that the confession equivalent to the belief in Christ's resurrection is the confession, 'Jesus is Lord'. 'Lord' was one of Paul's favourite titles for Christ. It was seen as the consequence of God's exaltation of Christ to God's right hand: Psalm 110:1 was a much reflected-on text (e.g. Acts 2:34; 1 Corinthians 15:25).

Calling upon the Lord

Paul has thus put Christ right at the centre of what he is setting over against the law (as understood by Israel), and he hastens to confirm the high status attributed to Jesus by the gospel in the preceding paragraph. Verse 11, 'All who believe in him shall not be put to shame', is a repeat quotation of Isaiah 28:16, already cited in 9:33, but now with Paul's favourite 'all' added. Since the exposition follows directly from verse 9, it is now clear that the stumbling stone is indeed Jesus, and that the Isaiah text calls for belief in this Jesus.

More important, for Paul it is precisely the exaltation of this Jesus as Lord which correlates with Paul's earlier attempt to demonstrate that there is no distinction between Jew and Greek (1:16; 2:9–10; 3:9). Paul could press the indictment against *all* flesh (3:20) as strongly as he did precisely because he believed that the one God of Jew and Gentile (3:29–30) had exalted Jesus from the dead to be Lord of *all*, and therefore able to respond to *all* who call on him (v. 12). The law as such had proved its inadequacy to reach effectively beyond Israel. It is Christ as universal Lord who finally surmounts the old division between Jew and Gentile.

The supporting text (v. 13) is quoted from Joel 2:32. As one of the Old Testament 'remnant' texts, it ties in well with the thought here (9:27–28 and 11:1–6). More striking, however, is the fact that 'the Lord' in Joel's text is, of course, Yahweh/God. This in fact is one of the most striking cases where an Old Testament text referring to Yahweh is referred in the New Testament to the exalted Jesus (cf. Philippians 2:11 with Isaiah 45:23). This amazing fact should not encourage the rather wooden deduction that Paul thought Jesus was Yahweh. But it is none the less significant that Paul could think of the one God operating so completely through this one Lord (cf. 1 Corinthians 8:6) that God's own role in salvation could be attributed to Jesus.

PRAYER

We praise you, O God, for the universal embrace of your concern and outreach in Christ. Grant us to share ever more fully in that breadth of vision and faith.

55 ROMANS 10:14–17

The UNIVERSAL GOSPEL

How faith happens

There is a straightforward logic in Paul's exposition. Faith is what God seeks in human beings above all else—that trust and dependence on him which Adam/humankind has failed to give (1:21), but which Abraham so fully exemplified (ch. 4). The law has failed to bring about and sustain that faith; Israel's response instead was 'works', which served simply to narrow the scope of God's saving concern (3:27–30; 9:30—10:5). But the gospel of Jesus Christ has proved a more effective medium for God's saving purpose: it fulfils Israel's own hope as expressed in Israel's own scriptures (9:33; 10:6–13); but it also reaches out to all with a universal appeal, and it brings about faith.

Paul cannot resist providing a kind of instruction manual. For faith to be exercised, it is necessary to know in whom faith is to be placed. That requires communication of the key information—about Jesus in this case—which in turn requires a preacher to be commissioned to tell about this Jesus (vv. 14–15).

Here clearly envisaged is a preaching which told of Jesus, in sufficient detail and with sufficient characterization for it to stimulate faith in him. That suggests something which scholars have been strangely loath to accept for some reason—namely that the substance and traditions now contained in the different Gospels would have been used in early preaching and teaching. It was what was proclaimed about Jesus—presumably his death and resurrection in particular, but other traditions as well—which generated faith.

This is a salutary reminder to all Christians—that Jesus stands at the centre of the Christian faith, not just for dogmatic or ecclesiastical reasons, far less for political reasons, but primarily because the story of Jesus proved so effective in causing belief. He stands at the centre of Christian faith not because theologians say so, but because countless thousands in the beginning (and since) came to faith through the gospel of Jesus. That fact must say something about basic Christian principles and priorities which have often been lost to sight.

Commissioned to preach

Also established by this passage is the importance of the preacher properly commissioned: 'How shall they preach unless they have been sent?' (v. 15). Here is recognized the importance of vocation: the task is so great, the responsibility so huge, that those undertaking it can hope for success only if they have been called and equipped from on high. Also in the background is the communal memory of the false prophets who have spoken in their own inspiration, or simply in order to be fed (Isaiah 28:7; Micah 3:5), and whose preaching has produced disruption rather than faith. That is also why a proper 'testing' of inspiration claimed has always needed to be part of the process of recognizing a vocation.

The Greek word 'send' (*apostello*) is the one from which 'apostle' comes. It was such a commissioning which lay at the heart of Paul's conversion and missionary work. Without implying that every preacher had to go through the same process as he, Paul nevertheless implies that a clear sense of commissioning was necessary. An ancient Jewish tradition affirms that 'the one sent is as the one who sends'; it is only a definite commissioning which enables the preacher to speak with the authority of the one who sends.

It is not surprising that the texts cited by Paul are from Isaiah 52—53. The text from Isaiah 52:7, 'How beautiful are the feet...' (v. 15) was quoted in other Jewish writings of the period. And the second text (v. 16) also comes from Isaiah 53:1, the beginning of the most famous passage regarding the Suffering Servant. Paul was deliberately plugging into one of the most cherished (if also puzzling) Jewish scriptures about the preacher of the gospel. It is precisely from these texts that the first Christians drew the term 'gospel' (the good news preached). Indeed, as the term 'apostle' similarly sums up the importance of the Servant being sent, so for Paul this passage pulls together two of the themes most fundamental to his own sense of mission—apostle and gospel. The apostle continues the mission of the Servant of God.

PRAYER

'How shall they believe in him whom they have not heard?
And how shall they hear without someone preaching?
And how shall they preach unless they have been sent?'
Send your apostles, O Lord, commission your preachers,
and let their words be with effect in begetting faith.

ISRAEL'S DISOBEDIENCE

The plot steadily clarified

As with chapter 2, in chapters 9—11 Paul slowly unveils the chief elements in his exposition. In chapter 2, what was not so clear at the beginning was *who* the object of Paul's indictment was; only in 2:17 did it become clear that he had in view the self-styled 'Jew'. In chapters 9—11, on the other hand, it is clear enough from the start who is in view—Paul's own people (9:3). What is not so clear is *why* Paul is so upset on their behalf. Hints have been given: 'only a remnant will be saved' (9:27), they have not reached the law (of righteousness), they have stumbled on the stone, their zeal is unenlightened, they have not submitted to God's righteousness (9:30—10:3).

But now Paul begins to speak more plainly. There are those who have 'not obeyed the gospel' (10:16, citing Isaiah 53:1), and the exposition makes it clear that it is indeed Israel in view, who have known (v. 19), but have refused to respond. And the paragraph climaxes with Isaiah quoted again and referred explicitly to Israel: 'All the day I have stretched out my hands to a disobedient and obstinate people' (v. 21; citing Isaiah 65:1–2). There is not simply failure and ignorance here but plain disobedience as well, culpable refusal to believe the gospel.

It is no surprise that Paul again quotes Isaiah (twice) on this point. For it is Isaiah who provided as near as the first Christians could find to the explanation of why Israel had rejected the gospel of their own Messiah. The answer, such as it was, came in Isaiah's own commission to preach, Isaiah 6:9–10: 'Go and say to this people, "Keep listening, but do not comprehend; keep looking, but do not understand. Make the mind of this people dull, and stop their ears, and shut their eyes... (lest they) turn and be healed."' We find this passage referred to quite often in the New Testament (particularly Mark 4:12; John 12:40; Acts 28:26–27), and Paul alludes to it again in Romans 11:8. The point is that Isaiah's own commission implied a recognition that, for whatever reason, the people would not listen or respond. This was part of his commission! The implication is that as for Isaiah, so likewise for the first Christians. And the deeper implication is that there is a hidden purpose of God in all this whose 'logic' will not become visible until it has been accomplished. The exciting thing for Paul at this point is that he thinks he has been given the key insight into the mystery of God's purpose for Israel.

Provoked to jealousy

Throughout this exposition in chapters 9—11, Paul has held two sides in tension: the one is Israel defined in traditional ethnic terms; the other is Israel defined in terms of divine call. Since 9:24 (though really since 9:6) he has been setting them out in parallel. Now he begins to show how they are interrelated. For the universal preaching of the gospel has in view not simply the spreading of the gospel to all Gentiles (v. 18). It has also in view that deeper purpose of God for Israel. For Paul, this is first signalled by the quotation from Deuteronomy 32:21: 'I will provoke you to jealousy by a not nation; by a senseless nation I will make you angry' (v. 19). This is one of the key pivotal moments in chapters 9—11. For in citing Deuteronomy 32:21 Paul is tying in the earlier talk of God as one who calls 'not my people' to be his people (9:25–26). But also he is deliberately anticipating the conclusion he is going to provide to the problem he himself is posing in 11:14, 25–26: as apostle, one sent to preach to the Gentiles (11:13), Paul seeks to win his own people by provoking them to jealousy when they see their own blessings (9:4–5) being given to others.

The play on the idea of being provoked to jealousy is worth noting, for 'zeal' and 'jealousy' are the same word. God is a 'jealous' God in relation to Israel; Israel had 'zeal', but unenlightened. And usually it was Israel who was said to provoke Yahweh to anger. Paul implies that the tables are turned: God will provoke Israel to a real zeal for him; God will provoke Israel to jealousy by his goodness to others. Such are the convolutions in God's relations with Israel caused by Israel's disobedience.

PRAYER

God, why is it that just when we think we have understood it all,
your purpose takes another twist and your grace astounds us
afresh? Forgive us our impertinence, and out of our humiliation
bring fresh cause for praise.

The REMNANT ACCORDING to GRACE

The precedent from scripture

Once again Paul follows the logic of his argument. The increasingly sharp criticism of Israel (10:16–21) points logically to the conclusion: God has rejected the people he first chose for himself! But once again Paul is not simply following human logic. He is dealing rather with the twists and turns of God's overarching purpose, celebrated in 8:18–39, but still seen only through the haze of human misunderstanding. Nor, it should be stressed, was this the first time the issue had been raised within Israel's history (e.g. Judges 6:13; 2 Kings 21:14; Psalms 44:9, 23; 74:1; Jeremiah 31:37; Lamentations 5:22; Hosea 9:17). Israel well knew, from its own history, how often by its own actions it had raised the very same question.

The fact that the question was so common within Israel's own scriptures means that Israel has been able to absorb it into its own life, even to celebrate it as a question to be answered with a firm 'No!' Paul follows suit: 'Not at all!' (v. 1).

The first reason offered by Paul himself, however, seems trite in comparison, even somewhat vainglorious—as though he was saying, 'No, because he saved me!' However, that would be a harsh reading. Paul is rather stressing his personal involvement in the issue (as in 9:1–3 and 10:1–2). More to the point, he is stressing his personal involvement as an ethnic Israelite, one of those referred to in 9:4; it is not as a believer in Christ Jesus that he speaks here, but as a descendant of Abraham and a Benjaminite. In all his reminder of what 'Israel' really means (9:7–13, 24), he is not letting go of the fact that Israel also has an ethnic identity. 'God has not repudiated his people whom he foreknew' (v. 2); his confidence in Israel's election remains unshaken (cf. 8:28–30).

Nevertheless, as might be expected, the main thrust of Paul's answer is an appeal explicitly to Israel's own scripture and history (vv. 2–4). The episode referred to is from one of Israel's darker periods, when the influence of Baalism had almost suffocated the worship of Yahweh. In that situation Elijah had even greater cause for despair over Israel. But God then revealed to him that there were 7,000 still faithful to him within Israel (1 Kings 19:9–18). In that remnant lay Israel's future and Elijah's reassurance of hope. It is perhaps to be noted that Paul does not appeal to the dramatic miracle of Elijah's victory on Mount Carmel, to which this episode is the sequel, but to the personal and private revelation which constituted Elijah's recommissioning.

By grace, and not works

From this, Paul is able to reply to the frightening charge of verse 1: this is a similarly dark episode in Israel's history; but as with Elijah, so now there was a remnant of Israel 'in the now time' (cf. 3:26). The point had already been made in 9:27–29, and is reaffirmed here from the Elijah story. Even in the darkest times, God does not leave himself without a witness—Elijah then, Paul now.

At the same time, Paul has no intention of ceding the ground he gained with such hard work when he pointed out what it is that constituted Israel as Israel. This was the main point of the initial stage of his argument in 9:7–13: that Israel is to define itself in terms of God's call and mercy, his election and grace, and nothing else. The very fact that Paul faced up to the difficult questions which that position pushed upon him (9:14–23) is an indication of how seriously Paul took this definition of Israel. A self-identification in terms of physical/racial descent would have been so much simpler.

The more enticing alternative was the one which had such influence in Israel's self-definition at the time of Paul—Israel identifying itself in terms of the works of the law, in terms of its obedience to the law. Paul here (v. 6) recalls the earlier argument of 3:20 and 3:27—4:5: that an emphasis on works narrowed the scope of God's grace to Israel; to boast in works was to boast in God as God of the Jews only. Israel's own theology of covenant was of a covenant between king and servant, God and human being, not between equals. So Israel should know well enough that it was a matter of grace; Paul repeats the word no less than four times in fourteen words.

PRAYER

'Grace'—that word again. A word to rest in when all else is puzzle and confusion. A fact to rely on when embarrassment and shame threaten to overwhelm. Thanks be to God for his uncalculating and uncomputable grace.

The ELECT & *the* REST

Remind me who the elect are

Paul's argument is beginning to become entangled again, so he pauses once more to sum up: 'What then?' (v. 7). His first summary point is the reminder that 'what Israel sought for, it did not obtain'. That is in clear echo of 9:31 ('Israel pursuing the law of righteousness has not reached the law'). But then he adds, 'The elect obtained it', again in echo of 9:30–31 ('Gentiles who do not pursue righteousness have attained righteousness'). So 'Israel' is different from 'the elect'? But then he adds what now appears to be a *third* category—'the rest'—who in context seem to denote the rest of Israel (who did bow the knee to Baal, 11:4). How do 'the rest' relate to both the preceding categories (Israel, and the elect)?

The confusion arises because Paul seems to have been playing two sets of couples off against each other. First, Israel as a whole is set over against the Gentiles in 9:30–33; Israel has somehow failed in respect of righteousness, whereas Gentiles have succeeded. Second, he seems to have distinguished, within Israel, between the remnant and the rest, both in 9:27–29 and in 11:1–5. So, who are the elect? Are they the remnant within Israel? The sequence of 11:7 following 11:1–6 would suggest so. But the near synonym used in 8:33 ('God's elect') clearly referred to all who have identified with Christ Jesus, which would certainly at least include Gentile believers. So, alternatively, are the 'elect' in view here the Christians, whether Jews or Gentiles? This would accord with the reminder that God's purpose operates in accordance with election, and not in view of what people do (9:11), and with the clarification of 9:24 that the 'called' include both Jews and Gentiles. So again we ask, who are the elect?

The answer seems to be that Paul does not want to choose between these alternatives. In particular, he does not want the issue to be reduced to questions once again of ethnic identity—either Jews or Gentiles, both Jews and Gentiles. That was precisely why, in chapters 9—11, he had shifted his main category from Jew/Gentile to Israel. In other words, he was seeking to re-establish a definition of Israel which is not simply identical with ethnic Israel, nor simply reducible to whether or not Israel's law is kept. Rather, Israel must always define and understand itself in terms of God's choice and purpose. And if that leaves the precise make-up of this Israel inexact for the present time—whether the remnant and/or Gentile believers—so be it.

The hardening of the rest

It is the last clause of verse 7 which would make many in Paul's audiences sit up. For he had already noted that the 'hardening' of Pharaoh was in contrast to his mercy to Israel (9:17–18). But now he talks of the hardening of *Israel*. Here at last the reason for Paul's earlier exposition becomes clear. It was not because he wanted to expound a doctrine of predestination, but because he saw that God's dealings with humankind always and inevitably have this two-sided nature. This fact was the key to what had been happening to his own people. He reminds his audiences of Esau as counterpart to Jacob/Israel, and of Pharaoh as counterpart to Israel's rescue from Egypt, because Israel is now filling the roles of Esau and Pharaoh.

The point is driven home by two stunning quotations. The first (v. 8) is from Deuteronomy 29:4, with probably a sideways glance to Isaiah 6:9–10. The Isaiah allusion in particular is a reminder that God himself has acted to prevent Israel from recognizing the course and character of God's purpose. The second (vv. 9–10) is from Psalm 69:22–23 with conflation from Psalm 35:8. Here, as in 3:10–18, Paul has taken a psalm directed against David's enemies and instead turned David's imprecations against his own people!

Paul evidently could not doubt that what was happening to his people was all part of God's purpose. He could not believe in a God of only good things and good times. The dark side of God had to be acknowledged, yes, and celebrated also. The even-handedness of God in dealings both good and bad, with Jew as well as Gentile, had to be affirmed. In doing so, Paul no doubt remained confident that God's final purpose was one of mercy (9:16; 11:28–32). But in the meantime the puzzle of the darkness could not be ignored.

PRAYER

There are days and nights of darkness when your face is withdrawn and your purpose seems perverse. Help us still to own you as God and to rely on you when we can see no way ahead and can make no sense of what you are allowing to happen to us.

59 ROMANS 11:11–16

The INTERDEPENDENCE of ISRAEL & GENTILES for SALVATION

The mood immediately lightens. Paul has posed the worst possible scenario he could imagine: God has set his face against Israel; that is what lies behind Israel's present stumbling (9:33; 11:9), blindness (11:8, 10) and disobedience (10:21). But that is not the end of the story. His solution to the puzzle of Israel's failure to function as Israel or to accept Israel's Messiah is twofold. First, Israel's stumbling is for the benefit of the Gentiles.

Israel's stumbling

Paul reverts to the image of a race (used in 9:30—10:4). Israel has stumbled, yes, but not sprawled on the racetrack, quite out of the race (v. 11). A stumble can be recovered from. The benefit of the stumble (though Paul now uses the term 'trespass') is that it gave the Gentiles time to catch up: salvation has come to the Gentiles (v. 11). Their trespass has meant 'riches for the world'; their failure 'riches for the Gentiles' (v. 12). Their 'rejection/throwing away' means 'reconciliation for the world' (v. 15).

What Paul has in mind, undoubtedly, is the sequence of events which saw a mission to fellow Jews by the first disciples of Messiah Jesus become a mission also to Gentiles. Acts provides a version of the story. Paul recognizes the hand of God in the fact that Israel on the whole turned its back on the gospel and the Jesus whom the gospel proclaimed. Were it not for that, the followers of Messiah Jesus might have stayed solely as a Jewish sect. Were it not for that, the impulse to take the gospel to Gentiles might have been limited in scope and success. This must be the one God's doing, enacting his purpose for the reconciliation of the whole world.

Paul is equally concerned that there should be no mistake among his Gentile audiences on this point also. It is not that the shift to the Gentiles marked a shift in God's purpose, from Israel to Gentiles. On the contrary, it was a continuation of the one purpose, which began with Israel (v. 16). The continuity between Israel and the wider Gentile world is that of first fruits to the whole—the first sheaf or batch set apart for God to ensure that all is consecrated. Alternatively, using the familiar image of a tree, it is the quality of the root which ensures the quality of the tree as a whole. In both images Paul is stressing that the Gentile Christians cannot understand themselves except in continuity with the Israel (the patriarchs) of old.

The world's reconciliation

The second phase of the grand scenario Paul sketches out is that the gospel's success among Gentiles will rebound on Israel by provoking Israel to jealousy at the sight of its own blessings (9:4–5) being so richly experienced by Gentiles. Indeed, Paul actually indicates that this was part of his own strategy. As 'apostle to the Gentiles' (v. 13), Paul did not see his mission as solely to the Gentiles—as he might (cf. Romans 1:5; Galatians 1:16). No, he deliberately glorified this very ministry in order to provoke his own people to jealousy (the word already signalled at 10:19), in the hope of saving at least some (v. 14). This fits with Paul's theological priorities as outlined particularly in the beginning of this letter—'Jew first, but also Gentile' (1:16). The point is that Paul saw God's purpose in terms of the interdependence of Jew and Greek, of Israel and Gentile, not as one people lording it over the other or bypassed in favour of the other.

Paul's vision is still richer. For he was evidently thinking in both global and eschatological terms. That is, he saw his mission as reaching out to embrace the whole world, and as prelude to the final achievement of God's purpose. If Israel's trespass meant riches for the world, what riches would Israel's 'fulness' (full number) mean (v. 12). If their rejection meant reconciliation of the world, then their acceptance would mean nothing short of life from the dead (v. 15), that is, the final resurrection (cf. 4:17 and 24). As in 8:19–23 Paul's vision of salvation encompasses the whole of creation, so here the same thought is spelt out to encompass the Israel that stumbled as well as the Gentiles who believed apart from the law.

PRAYER

What a vision of your wider purpose! Liberate us, good Lord, from the faith which is threatened by the announcement that God is concerned for the world as a whole, and help us to seek and to serve that wider purpose, in the spirit displayed here by Paul.

The OLIVE TREE *of* ISRAEL

This is one of Paul's most extended metaphors. The idea of likening Israel to a tree is a long established one (e.g. Psalm 92:12–13; Isaiah 61:3; Jeremiah 11:16; Ezekiel 17; Hosea 14:6), so it would not read strangely to anyone familiar with Israel's scriptures. No particular tree was specially associated with Israel, but the olive was one of the most valued trees in the Mediterranean region. To use it for Israel, therefore, was itself a reminder of how much God cherished Israel. It does not matter that Paul proceeds to envisage the most extraordinary tree-farming: grafting a wild shoot on to a cultivated tree was, of course, good and well-established practice; but the suggestion that old branches, cut off and withered, could themselves subsequently be regrafted in would hardly be seen as possible among olive farmers. Paul, however, is not concerned with good tree-farming. He bends the illustration to make his own point, and no doubt hopes that the astonishing character of what he suggests in everyday life will bring home more fully the miracle of God's purpose for ethnic Israel.

The metaphor was directed to Paul's Gentile audiences, as already signalled in 11:13 ('I am speaking to you Gentiles'). Having dealt so fully with his own people's presumption (2:1–29 and 3:27–30 in particular), he was all too aware that the Gentile Christians ran a similar risk. They might assume that the branches broken off were broken off in order to make room for them (the Gentile branches, v. 19). They might in consequence fall into the same trap of improper 'boasting' (vv. 18, 20). Paul's response is threefold:

- Gentiles were brought in to share the riches of Israel's heritage (v. 17).

- The gardener (God) determines who belongs to the tree and who is cut off; Paul recalls the two-sidedness of God's dealings (v. 22) already outlined in chapters 9—11 (9:13–23; 11:7–10).

- On the human side, it is only faith that sustains the graft (v. 20). That means that the branches already cut off can be grafted back on the same terms (v. 23); Paul obviously anticipates that unbelieving Israel will come to faith (11:26–27). But it also means that the new branches can in turn be cut off, if they cease to believe (vv. 21–22). It is precisely that boasting over others, that presumption of God's unquestioning favour, which is the very opposite of trust.

The warning here is unmistakable: continued relationship with God is a matter of faith responding to and trusting in God's kindness; without that trust and continued reliance, the relationship is broken.

The theology of Israel

This is one of the most powerful of Paul's expositions in its theological implications. First and foremost is the clarification it brings to Paul's understanding of Israel: he speaks of only one tree, one olive tree. He does not envisage the old tree of Israel being rooted up and replaced by another tree, the Church. Even the thought that the new branches have, as it were, taken over from the old, Paul repudiates in strongest terms: to start thinking in these terms is to follow ethnic Israel's failure ('boasting') and to ensure the destruction of the new branches. There is only one tree with which God has to do, only one Israel. Its roots are the patriarchs; some of its (ethnic) branches have been broken off, quite possibly in temporary fashion; others (Gentiles) have been grafted in, that is, grafted into Israel. The fact that the Church can be largely identified with the continuing and new branches does not mean that the Church has become the tree (or vice versa). The implications for Christianity's own self-understanding at this point are tremendous and have been insufficiently faced up to in the history of the Church.

Other points to note are the interdependence between faith and reliance on God's kindness, and between boasting and assumption of place and privilege. Paul here puts in summary form the fruit of his earlier exposition, particularly chapters 2—4. Also the clear implication remains that a believer can lose faith and and be cut off again— always with the further hope that unbelief will give way once more to faith. Paul's hope is particularly strong for the natural branches, his own people.

PRAYER

God, you are the tree-farmer who cuts off as well as grafts in. Cut off from me pride and presumption, lest they cut me off. Graft in faith and fear, that I may continue in your kindness. And evermore feed me from the rich root of Israel's heritage.

And SO ALL ISRAEL WILL BE SAVED

The mystery unveiled

Paul now brings his lengthy exposition in chapters 9—11 to a conclusion. The warning to the Gentile Christians in the Roman churches against falling into the same trap as the Jews of old had (11:17–24) enables him to return to the main thrust of the whole exposition. Why was it that Israel had stumbled and disobeyed with respect to the gospel of Messiah Jesus (9:33; 10:21)? How could God's word to Israel (9:6) still be trusted when this had happened? What did it say about his faithfulness and his righteousness? The answer has already been clearly implied: Israel (apart from the remnant) had suffered from God's hardening (11:7); they were suffering from the dark side of God's purpose of mercy, as Esau and Pharaoh had suffered in the past (9:13–18); for the present they were the objects of wrath rather than the objects of mercy spoken of in 9:19–23.

Paul sums up his claim as a 'mystery' (v. 25). This was a word rooted in Jewish apocalyptic to denote the heavenly secrets, particularly regarding the climactic future to this age of human history. The very term 'apocalypse' means an 'unveiling' of such mysteries to a chosen seer. For Paul, the supreme mystery was that of God's purpose for the world, in particular God's intention from the first to include at the last Gentiles with Jews as his people; or, as the point was subsequently elaborated, the mystery is Christ, in whom Gentile as well as Jew is united (Colossians 1:26–27; 2:2; 4:3; Ephesians 1:9–10; 3:3–6). By putting it as he does here, Paul probably intends his readers to understand that he himself had been privileged personally to receive the revelation of this particular mystery; and probably in answer to the anguish in the preceding paragraphs. How he received it, he does not say.

The mystery thus revealed was that 'hardening in part has come upon Israel until the full number of the Gentiles has come in' (v. 25). Paul confirms the harsh-sounding conclusion already reached (11:7–10). But he now qualifies it by adding 'in part'. Although Paul has drawn on the idea of a remnant (9:27–29; 11:2–7), his concern here is to maintain the thought of Israel as a single entity, suffering 'in part'.

Two covenants or one?

The triumphant outcome, towards which Paul has been driving since 9:1, 6, is that 'all Israel shall be saved'. 'Israel' here is the same 'Israel' about which he has just been speaking, ethnic Israel hardened in part. But more to the point, it is ethnic Israel in its true identity (9:7–13), ethnic Israel, but not Jews as exclusive of Gentiles (9:24). 'All Israel' will mean Israel as a whole, a people whose corporate identity and wholeness would not be lost even if there were some (or indeed many) individual exceptions.

The quotation from Isaiah 59:20–21 (vv. 26–27) is another form of the promise of a new covenant (Jeremiah 31:31–34), that is, of the covenant renewed. Some see this as envisaging two different ways of salvation—one for Jews, and one for Christians. On this interpretation, the Jews could look for final deliverance and forgiveness on the basis of their old covenant or their covenant renewed (cf. 9:4; 11:29); that is, their salvation would not be dependent on their believing in Christ (the original reference of 'the deliverer' in Isaiah 59:20 was almost certainly to Yahweh himself). In other words, salvation through Christ would only be for Christians and we would be confronted with the idea of two quite distinct covenants—one for Jews and one for Christians.

This is unlikely. Paul clearly regards the new covenant of Jeremiah 31 as operative for Christians (1 Corinthians 11:25; 2 Corinthians 3:3–6), and it is not at all likely that he would regard the reference in Isaiah 59:21 as pointing to a different covenant. And it is no more likely that he would think of a deliverer other than Jesus. Instead, he probably avoided making explicit the distinctively Christian character of his hope for Israel in order to avoid putting any Jewish readers off; he wanted his hope for Israel to be as wide as possible and the final appeal of the gospel to be as undistracted by Jewish/Gentile or Jewish/Christian tensions as possible.

PRAYER

There is a mystery about your dealings with humankind,
and with Israel in particular. Reveal to us what we need to
know and understand, so that our inter-religious dealings
may be informed by your deepest wisdom rather than by
our ignorance or our prejudices.

62

The UNFATHOMABLE GOD

Human disobedience and divine mercy

Paul at last draws together the threads of his exposition, answering both the fear that God has rejected Israel and the charge that God is open to severe criticism for his dealings with Israel.

The first answer is that there are two roles for Israel. On the one hand, there is the Israel which is hostile to the gospel; on the other, there is the Israel beloved of God on account of the patriarchs (v. 28). These are not two separate Israels, but two aspects or phases of God's dealings with one and the same Israel. Israel itself is caught between the phases of God's fuller purpose. The tension between flesh and Spirit is also the tension between law and grace, and also the tension between disobedient Israel and the Israel of God's mercy.

What is now clear for Paul is that Israel's phase of hardening 'in part' (11:25) is a temporary phase with a view to the gospel being extended to Gentiles too. But Paul never wavers from the conviction that God's original calling of Israel remains unchanged and has not been revoked (v. 29). His apostleship to the Gentiles (11:13) remained as his own primary calling, but he never ceased to be concerned for his own people and to believe that they were still central within God's purpose of mercy.

What has become more evident for Paul is that there is a strange rhythm in God's dealings with Israel, where the separate chords of human disobedience and divine mercy strangely combine to provide a wondrous harmony. What had been unclear before is that both chords combine in Israel's history—not just mercy but also disobedience, not just divine mercy but also divine hardening. Both are necessary to explain Israel's history, to explain the mystery of God's purpose. The dark side of disobedience and hardening is also part of that purpose, as much as the lighter side of divine grace and mercy. And this is true not just for Israel, but for God's dealings with all (v. 32). At the same time, Paul remains convinced that Israel's experience of God's mercy (9:15, quoting Exodus 33:19) is the key to understanding that God's dealings with all are fundamentally motivated by mercy: '...in order that he might have mercy on all' (v. 32).

The ultimacy of God

The thought of the last paragraph draws from Paul one of the great doxologies of scripture. It is motivated by this overarching thought of God's mercy (reiterated four times in vv. 30–32). But in the final doxology this thought is embedded within a profound sense of God's inscrutability. Rather like Job (Job 38:1—42:6), Paul recoils somewhat at the end of his extended attempt to make sense of God's dealings with Israel (verses 33–35 are a mesh of Old Testament allusions, most explicitly of Isaiah 40:13 and Job 41:11). Despite his disclaimer, he is after all in some danger of answering back like the clay pot: 'Why have you made me thus?' (9:20). For the reality is that the wisdom and knowledge of God are far beyond human criticism, the ways of God far beyond human comprehension (v. 33). It is in falling back into awed worship, in which God alone is glorified (v. 36), that Paul expresses most clearly the humble trust in God which, at the end of the day, is all that the creature can hope to offer to the Creator.

The final verse (v. 36) expresses a common thought in the religious writing of the time—the thought that all creation has a common source and purpose in God. The sequence of prepositions ('from, through, to') was particularly characteristic of the concern to leave nothing unattributed to God or outside his scope. Elsewhere Paul includes Christ in the thought (1 Corinthians 8:6; Colossians 1:16–17). But here Paul's concern is to focus exclusively on God alone. When talking of the sweep of God's purpose from beginning to end, it is the ultimacy of God which alone catches his attention; Christ is subsumed within that (cf. 1 Corinthians 15:24–28). And, best of all, the unfathomableness of God is the unfathomableness of the riches of his mercy, past all human comprehension and analysis.

PRAYER

O the depth of the riches and the wisdom and the knowledge of God. How unfathomable are his judgments and incomprehensible his ways… Because from him and through him and to him are all things. To him be glory for ever. Amen.

63   ROMANS 12:1

CHRISTIAN WORSHIP

What then follows?

Paul has now completed the main part of his exposition. He has strongly reaffirmed the righteousness of God as the principal feature of his gospel. By that he meant God's righteousness to all equally and impartially, though not forgetting that God has chosen Israel for a special role. It is a righteousness primarily determined by God's mercy, though Paul saw that the very same righteousness strangely included rejection and judgment within it (11:25–32). Now it is time to draw out the more practical consequences of this exposition.

Notice, first of all, the way he links his opening words into his argument. He appeals at once to 'the mercies of God'. Although the word used is different from that in 11:30–32, the two are near synonyms and the intention to link the thought back to that of 11:30–32 is evident. The appeal, in other words, is to the overarching purpose of God which has brought God's Israel and his gospel to this present situation. Paul remains supremely confident in God as the God of mercy; he advises his readers to live their lives in the light of that same mercy and not to act in any way that denies that mercy.

Second, the appeal to 'present your bodies' echoes the same language that Paul used in 6:13, 16 and 19. In chapter 6, Paul laid out the theological framework within which moral responsibility should be exercised. Here he begins to set out what that moral responsibility is likely to mean in practice for the Roman Christians.

Third, it is worth noting the interesting parallel with chapter 1. In 1:24–28 Paul had described human failure in terms of dishonouring bodies, worshipping the creature and 'disqualified mind'. Now he describes the very different character of Christian living in terms of presenting bodies, spiritual worship and 'renewal of the mind' (12:2). The implication is that the parallels are deliberate. The former phrases spoke of the failure of the old creation; here the elements which make up the new creation begin to come to expression. Here, in other words, is how the new creation will be lived out; here is the basis for responsible Christian living.

The sacrifice to be offered

One of the most striking features of verse 1 is the use of sacrificial language. 'Present' is itself the technical language of sacrifice, meaning 'offer or present a sacrifice'. That which is to be presented is explicitly described as a 'sacrifice', using the standard language for ritual sacrifice (*thusia*). 'Living' echoes the same imagery: the sacrificial animal was presented alive on the altar. 'Holy' maintains the same imagery, the sacrifice as essentially set apart to God. And the word for 'worship' always denotes temple worship in the Old Testament.

Why this concentration of sacrificial language? The obvious answer is that Paul wants his readers to understand that the worship 'acceptable, pleasing' to God is now not to be thought of as typified by, far less confined to, the Jerusalem Temple. Pleasing worship is not confined to a priest but is the responsibility of each believer.

And what is that different kind of sacrificial worship? Paul talks of 'offering your bodies as sacrifice'. By that he obviously does not mean, 'Offer an arm or a leg to God'. The phrase is equivalent to 'Offer yourselves' (as the parallel of 6:13, 16 makes clear). But he says 'bodies' presumably because he had in mind the fact that it is as embodied beings that we live: through our vocal organs we speak; through our legs we move; though our arms we act; and so on. We cannot communicate, except as 'bodies'. What is in view, then, is ourselves in our relationships, our day-by-day social intercourse.

If this is right, note what it means. Paul shifts the focus of acceptable worship from the sanctuary, and focuses it rather in the marketplace of daily living and communicating. It is here that Christian worship must display its character, here that discipleship will prove itself. It is in the quality of everyday relationships that God finds worship that is set apart and pleasing to him. What a striking way in which to begin his practical advice.

PRAYER

*O God, it is you who determine what should count as
'acceptable worship'. Teach us what should count as acceptable
worship for us, and help us to find and maintain the right balance
between what we do in church and what we do in our everyday
relationships and responsibilities.*

CHRISTIAN TRANSFORMATION

Conformation or transformation?

The contrast which Paul presents here is very insightful and instructive. In this present world there is constant pressure to conform to the trends and values of the times. It was no doubt true in Paul's day, but the point is clearly evident in today's world. Think of fashion—both the fashion pages of weekly magazines, and also the patterns of dress and informal dress-codes which become established among various age groups and social classes. But no doubt peer pressure and economic circumstances have always been considerable factors in shaping conduct and values. And no doubt, as now, so it was then, that the unconscious pressures were most effective. To follow the crowd, to go with the majority, is always likely to be the way of untruth, of failure to be true to ourselves and to what we know in our heart of hearts to be right.

If pressure to conform comes typically from without, the alternative posed by Paul comes typically from within. 'Transformation' is a word which characterizes Paul's understanding of the process of salvation. It is not something which can be imposed from without. Nor does Paul think of it in mystical terms, that is, in terms of some ecstatic rapture (hence 2 Corinthians 12:1–10). It is rather a transformation from within—from heart and mind to embrace the whole personality and daily conduct, ultimately including the body itself. Paul typically uses the present tense for the verb (as here): it is an ongoing process, indeed a lifelong process. Here too he thinks particularly of 'the renewal of the mind' as fundamental to the transformation of the whole person. As we shall see, and as a parallel like Titus 3:5 confirms, Paul will have been thinking of the Spirit as the power of renewal. The point is that a choice remains open to the believer, a choice for every day, whether to conform or whether to respond to the transforming power of God from within.

Discerning the will of God

What is at stake in all this is the high prize of all religion—to know and to do the will of God. The one who conforms to the world has forgotten: the highest good that the human creature can achieve is to do God's will. The one who seeks to be transformed by God is already asking the right questions and looking in the right direction.

Paul will certainly have intended his readers to recognize a contrast with what he wrote in 2:18. There he was characterizing the 'Jew' who was confident that in the Torah (the law) he had all that he needed to 'know God's will and to approve the things that matter, being instructed from the law'. To 'approve' the things that matter is the same word as Paul uses here, to 'discern' the will of God. The difference was this: the 'Jew' was confident that the law told him what to do. In many cases, he could read off the will of God from the law; hence, no doubt, the concern of Paul's fellow Pharisees to discuss all the various circumstances that any particular law might cover. What Paul now envisages is evidently a much more spontaneous 'discerning' process, where the renewed mind does not depend entirely on being schooled by some rulebook, but is itself enabled by God to discern directly what it is that God wants.

Of course, Paul would not intend the two alternatives to be driven to an outright antithesis—as though ethical decision could only arise from each new circumstance wholly independent of previous experience. The degree to which Paul's own ethical counsel drew heavily on scripture and the previous experience of God's people (see, e.g., 12:14–21) should scotch any such line of reflection. Nevertheless, we should retain as a matter of central importance Paul's portrayal of decision-making processes which depend primarily on waiting before God, on allowing the (corporate) renewal of the mind to work on the problem in view, rather than on looking primarily to precedent and approved practice. 'Discerning' is understood by Paul as a gift of the Spirit (cf. particularly Philippians 1:9–10 and 1 Thessalonians 5:21), never to be taken for granted, never to be simply assumed, but always to be sought with prayer and in humility.

PRAYER

Grant us, O Lord, that most precious gift of your Spirit,
that renewal of our attitudes and thought processes, so that we
may know what is the right thing to do despite the cacophany
and confusion of conflicting advice.

The BODY *of* CHRIST

Christians' corporate identity

The opening two verses set the tone for all that follows in the next four chapters. Paul is mindful, not least, that he has been shaping a rather different concept of the corporate character of God's people. But if God's people are no longer to be identified with a particular nation, if birth and distinctively Jewish practices like circumcision and sabbath no longer mark out the people, then how are they to be identified?

Part of the answer has already been given in 12:1–2: God's people are identified by the sacrificial commitment of bodily relationships (no longer by a particular temple ritual), and by discernment of God's will (no longer determined primarily by Torah). Now Paul provides the overarching corporate image: God's people are to identify themselves as the body of Christ, no longer as a nation distinctive from other nations.

Paul approaches the subject by recalling one of the main lessons to emerge from his previous exposition. If his audiences in Rome are properly to understand themselves as the body of Christ, they must turn their backs on the attitudes which had been so destructive of Israel's status before God (2:17–24), and which were equally in danger of undermining Gentile belonging to the olive tree of Israel (11:17–24). The first expression of the renewed mind (12:2) will be the ability to assess our own standing before God and to recognize on what it depends. Conformity to the world (12:1) involves an acquisitive ambition and a readiness to do others down in the struggle for personal advancement. The person being transformed by God's grace recognizes honestly the strengths and weaknesses of his or her own character (v. 3). By 'measure of faith', most think Paul refers to the standard or yardstick of faith. But it is more likely that Paul had in mind the individual's faith and trust seen as something enabled by God, as something very individual and personal.

Charismatic community

Here, as in 1 Corinthians 12, Paul takes up the familiar image of the human body for a city or state. The point of comparison is that a human body has many different parts or organs, and not all of them have the same function (v. 4). It is the very diversity of these organs and functions which makes the body one. The obvious lesson for the guilds and ethnic groups which made the city was that they needed to cooperate for the good of the whole. So with the Christian community: 'one body in Christ, and individually parts of one another' (v. 5). And the lesson is the same: the Christian community is characterized by relation to Christ, and its successful existence depends on members' mutual interdependence functioning as such.

In this case, the members of the body are defined as 'having charisms' (gifts, v. 6). As organs have functions within the body, so Paul conceives of members of the body of Christ as having some gift or function within the Christian community. As Paul would not conceive of any organ of the human body lacking a function, so he does not conceive of an individual believer lacking some part in the body's functioning. We could say that Paul understands all the members of the body as 'charismatics', if the term was not likely to mislead some. The point is that he did not see a Christian community as divided between those to whom ministry had been committed and those only ministered to. For Paul, all had ministry of one kind or another. And if any did not exercise that ministry, the whole body/church would suffer. All this is elaborated in 1 Corinthians 12:14–27.

This is where the concept of 'all-member ministry', or of 'the ministry of the whole people of God', comes from. The concept has been rediscovered in recent years, but is still bedevilled by the assumption that the practice of ministry starts from the sharp distinction between 'ordained' ministry and what is commonly, but most misleadingly, called 'lay' ministry. 'Lay' ministry is what Paul is talking about here —the ministry of the *laos*, of the people. As each must offer the priestly sacrifice of daily living (12:1), so each must minister for the good of the whole.

PRAYER

We thank you, Father, for that community to which you join us
in faith, one body in Christ. Help us to recognize what it means
to be a member of such a body, and grant us the grace
to serve you in others as you commission us.

HAVING GIFTS *that* DIFFER

Gifts of speaking and doing

The charisms/ministries which Paul mentions (vv. 6–8) were hardly intended as an exhaustive list. The various other lists drawn up elsewhere (1 Corinthians 12:8–10, 28; 14:26; Ephesians 4:11–12) indicate a significant overlap, but they also indicate a significant variation, best explained as Paul thinking up examples particularly appropriate to the audience to whom he was writing. In this case 'ministering' is left vague, presumably to cover a variety of ministries: 'he who exhorts' overlaps with 'prophecy' (1 Corinthians 14:3, 31); the last three examples here are not easy to distinguish. The gifts fall into two broad categories—speech and action.

By 'prophecy' we should not simply think of 'forth-telling' or 'preaching', as though all preaching was prophecy. 'Prophecy' would not be so called unless it were *inspired* speech. For Paul, that did not mean ecstatic, uncontrolled speech, as in some other cases; it is clear from Paul's careful treatment in 1 Corinthians 14 that prophecy for him was wholly rational speech, in some distinction from *glossolalia* (tongues). It could be counted a gift of the Spirit, however, because as human speech it was dependent wholly on the Spirit and not understood as humanly contrived speech.

Teachers were important persons in ancient communities. In an age where communication was characteristically oral, a community needed some who took the responsibility to learn and 'store' (in their minds) and pass on the community's traditions. 'Teaching' for Paul, however, could not be reduced to the mechanical passing on of tradition. This too is a gift, not least because tradition had to be interpreted as well as taught, and interpretation needed something at least of the same inspiration as prophecy. Note the balance between prophecy and teaching: prophecy is particularly open to new revelation and insight; teaching is more concerned to preserve what is important of what has already been recognized as revelation. Bearing this in mind, it is noticeable that Paul always regards prophecy as the more important gift (cf. 1 Corinthians 14:1). With teaching, a community will not die; but without prophecy, it will not live.

Of the last three charisms/gifts (v. 8), the first and the third look like examples of early Christian 'welfare service': 'he who shares... he who does acts of mercy'. And certainly earliest Christianity stood out within contemporary society for the care it exercised for its members, particularly subsequently in the setting up of hospitals. Here we see that the community of the Spirit was marked out by mutual concern one for another (cf. 1 Corinthians 12:25–26). The second of the three, however, could mean either 'he who leads' or 'he who cares'. Rather than deciding between the two, the more important point would be to emphasize that an essential characteristic of leadership was care for those whom one had been called to lead.

Charismatic constraints

In each case Paul offers some sort of qualification to the exercise of the ministry gift (cf. 1 Corinthians 12:10; 14:27–32; 1 Thessalonians 5:19–22). In doing so, he probably recognized the temptation to assume authority and status wider than the ministry itself. In most cases here, Paul's point is that the exercise of ministry should be limited to the ministry itself—service in serving, teacher in teaching, and so on. In particular, prophecy should be 'in proportion to faith'. That may mean 'in accord with the faith taught by the gospel/church'. But more likely it refers to the prophet's sense of inspiration: they should speak only so long as they consciously trusted in the Spirit to give them the words to say; beyond that they should cease (cf. 1 Corinthians 14:29–32).

Worth noting also is that the ministry in view is not some ability or even latent gift within the individual believer. It is the actual prophecy itself, the act of service. Paul seems to be concerned to emphasize that the gift is not to be understood as a human possession or talent; it is rather a gifting, an enabling to minister in a particular instance by the grace that comes from God.

PRAYER

We thank you, O Christ, for the diversity of ministries
with which you have gifted the communities of those who call
upon your name. Help us to recognize and encourage that diversity
so that the church may be ever active and ever more effective
as your body in the world.

ALL YOU NEED IS LOVE

Let love be sincere

Verse 9 begins a more disconnected sequence of exhortations. But the thought flows directly from Paul's preceding talk of the charismatic body and the importance of maintaining discernment in all matters charismatic. The hint is given in the talk of 'hating the evil, devoted to the good'. For this is more or less how Paul described the process of testing spiritual gifts (prophecy in particular) in 1 Thessalonians 5:19–22: 'Do not despise prophecy, but test everything, hold to the good, and avoid evil of every kind.' So the exhortations which follow give some indication of how a congregation might discern whether words or actions which claimed to be inspired were indeed charisms of the Spirit. For example, did they promote family affection, persistence in prayer, concern for hospitality?

In a word, did they promote love? It will be no accident that 12:9 follows 12:3–8 as 1 Corinthians 13 follows 1 Corinthians 12. The acid test of all claims to ministry is whether love is expressed and advanced thereby. The fact that Paul does this in both of his main discussions of the charismatic body indicates that he was well aware of the way callings can go to individuals' heads. The charismatic strand of Christianity which has surfaced repeatedly in Christian history is no stranger to the phenomenon of the prophet become guru become leader become dictator. Paul's key test for the reality of charism, as gift of grace, as ministry of the body of Christ, is therefore highly appropriate: does it display love? If not, there is a real question as to whether the claimed charism partakes more of 'what is evil' than of 'what is good'.

The other point worth noting is that 'genuine love' functions as a sort of headline. Indeed, the sequence from 12:9–13 is written almost as a series of brief notes, elaborating the headline: 'genuine love: hating the evil, devoted to the good; family affection in brotherly love for one another...'. This is what genuine love involves. And the whole sequence climaxes in the powerful call to love of neighbour in 13:8–10. In other words, the whole of Christian conduct must be inspired by genuine love, without play-acting, from start to finish.

How love acts

Paul's concept of love in practice includes, high among its expressions, 'family affection and brotherly love'; the doubling of the emphasis reinforces the point (v. 10). But that can be spelled out also in terms of 'showing the way to one another in respect'. That there can be respect without love is all too evident; but can there really be love without real respect for the other?

For the second time within a few verses (12:8, 11), Paul uses the word 'eagerness, earnestness, diligence, zest'. Here he calls for a love which is 'not negligent in eagerness'; love in its display should not be a drudgery or a bore, but vital and animating; presumably Paul knew his own share of individuals whose do-gooding stifled rather than stimulated love. In a similar tone he calls for a love which is 'aglow with the Spirit'—the imagery being of water heated and bubbling, or of a 'burning' passion; the action of the Spirit in a life Paul expected to engage the emotions and deeper feelings. Such deeply felt emotion would enable a more sustained service of the Lord.

'Rejoicing in hope' and 'steadfast in affliction' recall the expositions of 5:2–5 and 8:17–25. 'Persisting in prayer' recalls the climax to Paul's earlier exposition of the Spirit (8:26–27).

Paul never allows the thought to narrow down to an individualistic piety. He remains constantly aware of the corporate dimension of faith through love. So here (v. 13) he reminds his readers of the supremely religious responsibility of hospitality. In the ancient world this was of major importance, since inns were often held in bad repute. Neither Jesus nor Paul could have carried through their missions without being able to depend on it (cf. e.g. Mark 2:15–17; 6:8–11). The grace of hospitality is something which needs to be recovered.

PRAYER

Lord, grant us grace, grant us ministry, but, above all, grant us love. Grant us that love which engenders respect, which nurtures healthy relationships, which adds zest to community living, and which builds up your body.

68 ROMANS 12:14–21

LIVING *in* DIFFICULT TIMES

The modern reader of Romans should never forget that the letter was written to what were probably small house churches scattered through much of the capital city of the Roman Empire. Here, above all, we need to appreciate how vulnerable these little house churches were. The Roman authorities were very suspicious of clubs and associations, lest they should become a focus for unrest or even treachery against the State and its officials. There was a tradition of favour being shown to synagogues, as the respected religious institutions of a particular national minority within the major cities of the Empire. But how did the new Christian groupings stand in legal terms? Were they to shelter under the synagogue legislation, or present themselves as legally equivalent to friendly societies, or take the risk of being reported as potentially dangerous factions?

It is against this threatening background that the next two paragraphs have to be understood, particularly the talk of persecution, evil, vengeance and enemy. We today hardly need reminding that minority groups in large cities can often find themselves the butt of ill-humour, the focus for petty trouble-making. Given that this is so, how should those likely to be victimized prepare themselves and handle themselves? Paul draws on two sources of wisdom and counsel.

Inherited wisdom

The many Jewish groups scattered through the Roman Empire and Babylonia had long experience of living under foreign and often suspicious rulers. Valuable lessons of that experience had been recorded in Israel's scriptures and writings, and it is worth noting how much of 12:14–21 echoes these traditions: compare verse 15 with Ecclesiasticus 7:34; verse 16 with Proverbs 3:7 and Isaiah 5:21; verse 17 with Proverbs 3:4; verse 18 with Psalm 34:14; verse 19 with Leviticus 19:18 and Deuteronomy 32:35; verse 20 with Proverbs 25:21–22.

Equally striking are the many echoes of Jesus' teaching. Verse 14 contains one of the strongest allusions to the Jesus tradition outside the Gospels (see Matthew 5:44; Luke 6:27–28) and is probably intended to set the keynote for the verses that follow (12:14—13:7). It is notable how many echoes there are in this part of Romans of the central section of the 'Sermon on the Plain' in Luke 6 (cf. v. 14 with Luke 6:28; 12:17, 21 with Luke 6:27–36; note also 14:10; Luke 6:37). Quite possibly Paul knew this very material which Luke was later to collect in his Gospel.

The wisdom of the oppressed

The most striking feature of the resulting counsel is the positive, outgoing goodness called for in response to the intimidation and petty malice often likely to be directed against Christians in such circumstances. Paul does not advocate a policy of resistance, even of passive resistance. No doubt this was in large part a matter of prudence: a reputation for good neighbourliness and kindliness might well help ensure the support of the citizenry at large in any confrontation with the authorities. More to the point, perhaps, Paul would also have in mind the impact which such response would have in impressing neighbours and workmates. The evangelistic effects of witnessing how Christians conducted themselves under persecution were an important element in the early expansion of Christianity.

Most to the point: this was the way Christians should live with others, both fellow Christians and others. Paul does not make a sharp distinction between the two groups in this passage. This counsel still comes under the headline of 'genuine love' (12:9); here is an example of how love reacts under provocation (cf. 1 Corinthians 13:4–7). Also important is the fact that Paul does not expect his readers to withdraw from those situations where they were liable to be provoked and persecuted. This is guidance not on how to avoid persecution but on how to live through it in a positive way.

At the same time Paul was clearly aware that persecution often stirs up feelings of deep anger which have to be expressed (v. 20). He does not doubt that some sort of vengeance is called for. He points out, however, that appropriate vengeance is something only God can dispense (v. 19). Christians should leave it so and try instead to overcome evil with good (v. 21).

PRAYER

Lord, we pray for those who suffer persecution for their faith. Enable them to meet such persecution with blessing and without bitterness, to trust in your fairness, to resist evil and to overcome evil with good.

LIVE *as* GOOD CITIZENS

Political realities

This passage has been regarded for centuries as the charter for church–State relations. Above all it seems to authorize the State and state officials as ordained by God and to require unquestioning subjection to their authority. It is this passage which gave the Middle Ages their favourite portrayal of Paul as bearing a sword, because it was Paul (v. 4) who was understood to legitimate capital punishment in a Christian State and the exercise of state power in the service of the church. The modern tradition of Western democracy, mindful of the too-frequent parallel traditions of political corruption and tyranny, finds such a call for unquestioning subservience impossible to accept in any straightforward way. It is important, therefore, to set Paul's forthright advice in its historical context.

For one thing, we should recall that Rome's government of its conquered provinces was on the whole beneficial; its empire could not have lasted so long otherwise. Diaspora Jews in particular had benefited overall from benevolent rule for the last hundred years, with special privileges to practise their religious traditions reaffirmed and protected by successive rulers. Paul's language here reflects such good experience. The first Christian groups were probably able to shelter under that benevolence initially, although their ambivalent status was always likely to be called in question, and it was only a few years later (AD64) that Emperor Nero chose to blame them for the fire in Rome in a horrendous persecution.

The other point worth remembering is that the reality of politics at that time was as far removed from democratic tradition as we can imagine. Those who start by querying the sort of counsel Paul gives need to remember first that such querying was an impossibility for Paul himself. Political power rested with a relatively small and wealthy élite, exclusively male, and for those outside these circles to voice criticisms of the system was to invite an abrupt demise. Those who belonged to ethnic minorities, to new religious sects (always viewed with deep suspicion in Rome), consisting in a large number of slaves or non-citizens, were undoubtedly wise if they kept their heads down and lived quiet, law-abiding lives—and, not least, paid the taxes levied by the State! Paul in effect counsels: since you cannot change the terms under which you live, and since your position is already hazardous, remember the political realities of the politically power-less, and live accordingly. It will thus be evident that Paul's thought flows directly from 12:14–21 into 13:1–7.

Under God

So Paul does provide a theology for the State. God wills an orderly society; it is right for some to bear authority over others, for that is how orderly society is achieved and maintained. A healthy society will have an element of fear (at the penalty for wrongdoing), it will de-pend on its members listening to the voice of conscience, and it will provide a means of honouring those to whom honour is due. Such a rationale still applies in contemporary society.

Paul, however, will hardly have been unaware that government and rulers often did become corrupt, and members of society would often suffer unjustly at the hands of corrupt officials. It is equally important, therefore, to note that Paul sets his vision of orderly government under the rubric, 'under God'. Note the repeated phrases—'given by God', 'established by God' (v. 1), 'ordinance of God' (v. 2), 'God's servant' (v. 4, twice), 'ministers of God' (v. 6). Paul's treatment here not only provides divine warrant for government, it also serves as a reminder to government of its own answerability to higher authority. Implicit in all this is that what is in view is good government. And where government transgresses the limits of good government, it transgresses the limits of its God-given authority. In Paul's situation, that could not be taken as encouragement to rebellion; the appropri-ate attitude was rather that of 12:14–21. But in the different political circumstances of today, Paul's counsel can serve as the basis for democratic critique of abuse and lobbying for change.

PRAYER

*Almighty God, we acknowledge before you that as social creatures
we need to have structures and order by which and within which
to live. We thank you for the gift of good government. Help us
ever to promote and support it, and ever to remind those who bear
authority of their responsibility before you.*

LOVE YOUR NEIGHBOUR

The law summed up

Paul makes an interesting, if slightly awkward transition from his counsel on State and taxation. The only debt which we should have to others is the debt of love, 'to love one another'. In this way he returns to what is the central theme of his exhortation (12:9)—to love one another. The pragmatic counsel of cautious good citizenship (never get into debt) is overtaken by the positive ideal of outgoing concern for the neighbour.

It is important to note that Paul sees his counsel as reaffirmation of the law. Fulfilling the law was still important for him (he repeats the point). For all the misgivings he had about the way the law was abused in his own religious tradition, he still affirms its importance as a measure of what God looks for in living the good life (cf. 3:31; 8:4). Only such an emphasis will be sufficient to enable the Roman Christians to follow the demanding advice of the preceding paragraphs. The orderliness of good citizenship and effectiveness of harmonious community will only be fully sustainable if love of neighbour is the dominant consideration in all policy and decision-making.

It is also important to appreciate that Paul was not doing something unusual in summing up the law in this way. The most often cited parallel is that of Hillel, Jesus' elder contemporary. Hillel had summed up the law in the negative form of the golden rule: 'That which you hate, do not do to your fellows'. And the great rabbi Akiba, from the generation following Paul, spoke of the same verse (Leviticus 19:18) as 'the greatest general principle in the Torah'. With so many laws, conflict of counsel would often be inevitable. So it was highly advisable to order priorities to help decide when practical advice was confused. Jesus had so advised (Mark 12:28–31) and the accounts of his handling of such as the sabbath day disputes (Mark 2:23—3:5) show how he himself lived out that advice. Undoubtedly Paul owes his own counsel at this point to the tradition of Jesus' own teaching.

In this case Paul cites also the seventh, sixth, eighth and tenth of the ten commandments (against adultery, murder, stealing and coveting). By so doing he indicates how focusing on the love commandment as the primary norm for conduct works for himself. It does not become an alternative to the law (it covers the commandments mentioned, but also 'any other commandment'). But also, by mentioning just these most basic commands governing social living, he gives his own example of how the love command functions in cases where particular commandments run counter to love of neighbour. There is a loving which seeks the good of the other without necessarily being bound by convention and which fulfils the requirements of God's law more effectively than conduct determined primarily by legal precedent.

A specific love

The love command is often expounded in a way which makes its fulfilment either impossible or else so vacuous as to rob the command of all its effect. So it is worth noting the limitations which the formulation drawn from Jesus puts upon the command.

For one thing, the command to love is limited to 'the neighbour'. That, of course, does not mean simply the person literally next door —though it certainly includes the person next door! Jesus' parable of the good Samaritan (Luke 10:25–37) made it clear that God may give anyone to be a neighbour—if the half-breed heretic Samaritan, then certainly the refugee or asylum seeker or impoverished Third World peasant. Yet, at the same time, it is the neighbour that we are speaking of, not the whole world. In specifying the neighbour, but not who the neighbour might be, Paul helps to keep the love offered as practical but not restricted by artificial boundaries of geography or precedent. The neighbour is the specific person whom we encounter in the course of daily life, who has a need we can meet. It is not possible to regulate such good neighbourliness by rules or restrictions.

For another, Paul echoes Jesus in also specifying that the neighbour should be loved 'as yourself'—not more than ourselves or beyond our resources. The most effective neighbourly love arises from and expresses a realistic self-esteem. In contrast, a vague, all-embracing love for the world does not actually love others as we love ourselves.

PRAYER

Lord, we thank you for the grace of love. Help us to love, really and realistically. Show us day by day who is our neighbour, and enable us to love our neighbour as ourselves.

A SPUR to GOOD LIVING

Paul has achieved a surprisingly comprehensive instruction for practical living, to his audiences in Rome, both as individual members of the various churches gathered for worship (12:1–13) and as individual members of a wider society of which they were still a part (12:14—13:10). But he evidently felt it necessary to round off this ethical teaching by reminding them of the eschatological realities within which they lived, thereby injecting a note of urgency into his counsel.

Wake up

It is important to recall that Christianity began with something of an eschatological fever. *Eschaton* denotes the end, the climax and fulfilment of God's final purpose for his creation and people. Jesus had spoken of it under the image of 'the kingdom of God', and still Christians pray for that kingdom to come, as Jesus first taught. With the resurrection of Jesus, his first disciples saw the beginning of the end, the pattern for the final resurrection. They evidently expected the new age marked by Christ's resurrection to be soon consummated by Christ's own return in glory. They understood the Spirit they now experienced as the further mark of the new age, the last age.

This is the atmosphere Paul breathes here. He expects his readers to recognize 'the time' (v. 11), the present as the space within which God has acted decisively in and through Jesus. Hence immediately the thought of a time which is short and diminishing: the dawn is coming; wake up and get ready to live as those who belong to the day. By such imagery Paul seeks to motivate his audiences for the realities of their daily life.

It is equally important to recognize the degree to which the *eschaton* has not been realized for Paul. The night is in fact still present (v. 12). The conditions more typical of the old age are still in full flood— 'revelry and drunkenness, debauchery and sexual excess, quarrelling and envy' (v. 13); the echoes of 1:24–31 will not be accidental. More to the point, the Christians still need to be counselled to 'put off (such) works of darkness' (v. 12).

All this reflects Paul's double conviction that there is a process of salvation which has been given a decisive beginning 'when we believed' (v. 11), but which has yet to be completed, which still requires self-discipline on the part of the believer (cf. e.g. 5:1–5, 9–10; 8:9–11). The difference between night and imminent dawn may not be very clear as yet, but their conduct should already reflect the day much more than the night.

The modern reader inevitably asks: how does the fact that Christ has not yet come again change the force of Paul's counsel? It may unavoidably diminish the note of urgency. But otherwise it need affect Paul's counsel not at all. For the differences between conduct of the day and conduct of the night are still clear. The process of salvation has still had a decisive beginning, renewed in every fresh conversion. And the need for resolution and discipline is as great as ever for those who are as conscious of night as they are of the day of God's fulfilled purpose to come.

Put on Christ

Verse 14 recalls all that was said in 8:9–13. It uses one of the powerful metaphors on which Paul drew elsewhere—the putting on of a character(istic) as one puts on a garment. It was used in theatre talk of the time: 'to put on Tarquin' meant 'to play the role, assume the character of Tarquin'. In Jewish tradition the same imagery was used in connection with the Spirit 'taking on' a person (as in Judges 6:34 and 2 Chronicles 24:20); and the later Pauline letters talk of 'putting on the new man' (Colossians 3:9–10; Ephesians 4:24).

Many see the image as specifically baptismal, on the basis of Galatians 3:27. But Paul was hardly calling for a rebaptism, and it is more obvious to see it as one of the various metaphors which Paul uses to describe the transformation that conversion brought about in the lives of individuals. Such commitment cannot be regarded as 'once for all' in the sense that it needs no renewal or reaffirmation. On the contrary, the implication is that it does need regular renewal, such are the threats of the night on the day. The flesh and its desires still need to be confronted (8:12–13).

PRAYER

*Grant, O God, the proper balance between our confident trust
and hope in you, and the urgency and discipline we need to ensure
the completion of your good work in us.*

RELATIONSHIPS *within the* CONGREGATION

Paul's instruction so far has been fairly general, apart from the specific advice on paying taxes (13:7). But now he raises a specific issue involving the attitudes of believers to each other. He spends nearly thirty verses on the subject (14:1—15:6), so it was obviously a matter of major concern and it is worth trying to clarify what was at stake.

The historical context

The precise situation can only be partially clarified. The main clue is given by the opening and concluding emphasis: 'Welcome the one who is weak in faith' (14:1); 'welcome one another' (15:7). The situation envisaged was therefore one where some members, the 'weak in faith', were feeling unwelcome. Paul seeks to counter this unloving trend in the wake of his previous advice (12:9—13:10).

Some years before, it is reported that Emperor Claudius 'expelled Jews from Rome because of their constant disturbances at the instigation of Chrestus' (Suetonius, *Claudius* 25:4). The report reads like a rather confused account of disturbances caused within the Roman Jewish community by early preaching on Jesus as Messiah/Christ ('Christus' would sound very like 'Chrestus'). Acts 18:2 in fact tells us that Priscilla and Aquila had had to leave Rome at that time. Probably, therefore, Jewish leaders of the new Christian house churches were among those expelled. After Claudius' death a few years later, his decree would lapse and no doubt Jews who been affected by it would begin to return to Rome. The scenario suggested by all this, then, is Gentile house churches who had become accustomed to ordering their affairs without much Jewish participation, and who now found their more Gentile pattern of communal living being called into question by the Jewish returners. It is some such resentment implied in the calls to extend a genuine 'welcome' that seems to lie behind Paul's principal concern in this section (14:1—15:6).

The issue

The issue at first seems fairly trivial within the larger scheme of things. Some felt unconstrained in what they ate; others avoided meat (v. 2) and wine (14:21). Some regarded particular days as special; others regarded no day as particularly special (14:5–6). Was it then simply a dispute about vegetarian practice or temperance or holy days? Why would Paul spend so much time on such issues here?

In fact, however, the underlying issue was very much more important. The key fact to appreciate is that the issue of clean/unclean food and the issue of sabbath observance had become fundamental to Jewish identity. As Leviticus 20:25–26 makes clear, the law of clean and unclean was the mirror of Israel's sense of set-apartness to God and from other nations. According to 1 Maccabees 1:62–63, the blood of martyrs had been spilled in defence of this basic conviction. Its importance for most Jews is well reflected in the scene in Acts 10, where Peter states emphatically, 'I have never eaten anything common [profane] or unclean' (Acts 10:14). In other words, the avoidance of unclean food was at the heart of Israel's identity as a people set apart to God. It is clearly this issue which is in view in Romans 14, where precisely this same vocabulary is used—'common (profane)', 'clean' (14:14, 20).

Similarly with special days, the sabbath in particular. Its equal centrality for Jewish identity as the people of God is reflected in various texts (e.g. Genesis 2:2–3; Exodus 31:16–17; Deuteronomy 5:15; Isaiah 56:6; Ezekiel 20:16). Many Jewish believers must have been stunned when their fellow Christian Gentile converts ignored the sabbath law in particular.

In other words, what was at issue in Romans 14 were not secondary questions of personal choice. On the contrary, these were convictions and traditions which were deeply rooted in Israel's self-consciousness. To call them in question was to call in question the most precious things that they had believed and practised. This is why the way Paul handles these issues is so instructive for all subsequent generations.

PRAYER

Help us, O Lord, to recognize that what is important to us may not be so important to others, and that what is unimportant to us may be of vital importance to others; and grant us the grace to recognize when the difference matters.

73

The DANGERS of UNRESOLVED DIFFERENCES

The parties involved

If the background outlined in the previous section is reasonably sound, there will be no real doubt as to who the parties involved in the disagreements of 14:2 and 6 were. The avoidance of meat (and wine) was a familiar Jewish practice to avoid any danger of transgressing the law of clean and unclean foods. And the regard for holy days probably has in mind a concern to observe the Jewish sabbath above all else; no other days would likely be counted as so important within Christian groups. Those who avoided all meat (v. 2), therefore, were probably the same as those who observed some days as special (14:6). These would be Jewish believers in particular (it was returning Jews who were probably feeling unwelcomed), though Jewish traditions had proved very attractive to many Gentiles, so such Gentile believers were probably also in mind.

Paul identifies the two parties as 'weak in faith' (v. 2) and 'the strong' (15:1). By the former Paul presumably means those who (in his judgment) were failing to trust wholly in God, in contrast to Abraham who was strong in faith (4:18–21). That whole exposition (Romans 3—4) also shows clearly what Paul had in mind. The 'weak in faith' were those who trusted in something other than God, or something additional to God. They trusted in God *plus* observance of food laws and sabbath; they made faith in Christ *dependent* on observance of such rules, as though there could be no real faith without such observances. In contrast, others, like Abraham (or Paul himself), trusted only in God and saw such faith as alone sufficient ground for relation with God through Christ.

The point is worth underlining. Many would find Paul's categorization surprising. Are not those who hold strongly to their traditional practices more accurately designated as 'the strong'? They have strong principles. Whereas those who do not have such firmly drawn guidelines for practice are better designated 'the weak'. But Paul is clear throughout this letter that faith alone is what makes the difference in the definition of a Christian and of Christian conduct. To add further requirements to faith alone is actually to diminish faith.

Faith alone

The centrality of faith in what the gospel looks for in human response is so important for Paul that it is worth underlining. He found he had to assert it in the face of even such fundamental issues as the traditions of food laws and sabbath. But such issues have repeatedly cropped up in Christian history. The list of issues on which Christians have disputed and divided is almost endless. One thinks for example of the sacraments—Lord's Supper, Eucharist, Mass—and baptism (infant or believers); or of episcopacy and papal primacy, or church polity, or scripture, or spiritual renewal, or women's minstry, or abortion, or human sexuality. In every case there have been those who have regarded the issue as definitive of Christianity.

To all these, Paul in effect gives the same message: the fundamental issue is that of faith. Do you trust in God through Christ? Do you trust in God alone through Christ, or do you also require assent to other articles of faith? Then, in so doing, you are actually weakening faith, not defending it. You are beginning once again on that downward slope which puts trust in things on a par with, or even in place of, trust in God alone (1:21).

Paul reinforces the point at the end of the chapter when he actually defines 'sin' in terms of faith: 'everything which is not of faith is sin' (14:23). In other words, faith, trust in God, should be the benchmark for conduct, not least on delicate or divisive issues. To act in a way which contradicts that basic trust is an act of self-condemnation (14:22–23). To count an issue which is additional to faith as of equal importance with faith is sin and destructive of Christian community. Ironically in Christian history, it is the very concern to protect and defend faith, by the more detailed confessions and creeds and rubrics and traditions, which have resulted in the divisions that Paul sought to avoid by his strong counsel in this chapter.

PRAYER

We praise you, O God, for the wondrous gift of faith. Forgive us for the way in which we tend to confuse it with other things. Help us to cling to the bare simplicity of trusting in you and you alone.

How These Christians Despise One Another!

The spectrum of faith

In every issue, particularly where it is perceived as of special sensitivity, there is a tendency on one side to claim the support of tradition, and the counter tendency to argue in some measure for departure from that tradition. In the case in point, 'the traditionalists' is a fair way of describing those who wished as a matter of first importance to maintain the traditions of clean/unclean and sabbath—whether Jewish believers or Jewish-attracted Gentile believers. The alternative position, which argued for freedom to live without reference to such traditions, could be called 'the liberals'. The term, unfortunately, has negative overtones for many—I say 'unfortunately' because the sense of liberation from past tradition is such a strong feature of Paul's own theology, and it is just that sense which is reflected in Paul's own attitude here (particularly 14:14, 17–18). What matters, however, is not so much the terminology but the recognition of a typical spectrum of Christian (or any) opinion on disputed issues as between those strongly attached to established tradition and those willing to sit loose to that tradition.

Paul provides a remarkable psychological insight in verse 3 when he warns of the dangers that Christian protagonists face in their attitudes to one another. 'Let not the one who eats despise the one who does not eat, and let not the one who does not eat pass judgment on the one who eats.' The danger confronting each in their mutual relations is not the same, as the different verbs used by Paul indicate. The danger confronting the more liberal (or, more accurately, those who perceive themselves as the more liberated) is that they '*despise*' the inhibitions of the more traditional, whereas the danger confronting the more traditional is that they '*condemn*' those who sit light to the traditions which they themselves prize so dearly.

It is not clear whether Paul considers either of the two dangers as more serious than the other for Christian community. To 'despise' fellow Christians might not seem so serious as 'condemning' them.

But in fact both are equally sins against the love of neighbour which is Paul's primary message through this section (chs. 12—15). And 14:10 also implies that despising and condemning easily merge into each other. Nevertheless, Paul addresses and rebukes first the weak and their attitude of condemnation of the strong (14:3–10).

Condemning the fellow believer

The threat to Christian community from the side of the weak, the traditionalist, is that they actually question the Christian standing of the strong, the more liberal. In this case, since the laws of clean and unclean were perceived by them as still fundamental to covenant relation with God, those who ignored or transgressed these traditions could simply not be accepted as Christian. Paul had confronted the same issue head on with regard to circumcision and whether Gentile believers needed to be circumcised. With the law on the point so clear (Genesis 17:9–14) there were many who simply took it for granted that unless Gentiles were circumcised they could have no place within the people of God (Acts 15:1). Paul's letter to the Galatians was a fierce resistance to this conviction (deeply rooted though it was in scripture), and this resistance has become itself an integral part of Christian scripture.

The point and principle Paul defends in these cases is one which needs to be clearly restated, since it has such breadth of reference to similar cases. There is a constant danger in Christian history of attempting to secure a pure church—the danger of defining Christian faith so precisely, and acceptable Christian conduct so narrowly, as to exclude others who believe but want to express their faith and to live differently; the danger of demanding conformity to a particular creed and form of worship. There is the danger, above all, of denying, explicitly or implicitly, the status of Christian to those we do not know, or do not like, or do not get on with, or cannot browbeat into agreement. There is a danger of denying the status of Christian to those who believe but will not conform.

PRAYER

*Forgive us, O God, for the way in which we so quickly condemn
and despise others who name the name of Christ. Grant us that
larger vision of faith that we might recognize it
and live within it more fully ourselves.*

75

The APPEAL *to the* WEAK

Paul confronts a situation in which more traditionalist groups within the Roman congregations were in danger of condemning others who sat more loosely to some of their most cherished convictions. The fact that the traditionalists were in a minority probably left them feeling under greater threat themselves and so all the more outspoken in their condemnation of other views and practices. It is noteworthy, then, that although the main thrust of Paul's exhortation is directed at the 'strong', he starts by rebuking the 'weak'.

Christ alone determines who is acceptable to him

Paul's first concern was to get the weak to accept the strong as fellow Christians. His chief argument is that *God* accepts people whose views and practices *they* regard as unacceptable. Paul presses the point with repeated emphasis: 'Let not the one who does not eat pass judgment on the one who eats, for God has welcomed him. Who are you who condemns the slave of someone else? In relation to his own master he stands or falls. And he shall stand, for the master is able to make him stand' (14:3–4).

This is the crucial first step in Paul's pastoral strategy—to get the more conservative believers actually to accept that someone who differs from them in something they themselves regard as crucial may nevertheless be acceptable to God. In other words, the weak must recognize that God is far bigger than their own conception of him. Their fault is actually the primeval fault of Adam (Genesis 3:5)—of seeking to be like God, to determine what is right and wrong for themselves.

The same urgent need is at the root of all denominational and ecumenical disputes. If each can accept the other as also Christian, as really and fully Christian, then the foundation for shared worship and mission is given. Without such genuine acceptance, only condemnation can result—and if not in public statements, then certainly in the privacy of meetings of the like-minded. It is unclear which is the more fatal for fellowship and community and the body of Christ.

Each must decide for oneself before God

Paul's second piece of counsel is that each should be fully convinced in their own mind on such contentious subjects which threaten congregational unity (v. 5). But that conviction should not be used to browbeat the other. My conscience is the measure for my conduct before God; it should not be used as a stick to beat my brother, whose conscience may speak differently. In other words, Paul recognizes that two Christians can disagree and yet both be right; it is not necessary for you to be wrong for me to be right.

This policy could sound dangerously libertarian and too individualistic for many. It is important, therefore, to recall that this is only the beginning of Paul's counsel on the whole issue. It is also important to note how Paul conceives this holding of opinions which differ from those of others on important matters. Verse 6 makes clear that these differing views have to be reached before their common Lord. Paul is able to assume that the disputants live out their differing patterns of conduct in honour of their common Lord and in thankfulness to God. Here is an interesting criterion for disputed conduct: can those who so act give thanks to God for that conduct?

Once again, then, we come back to the primary basis for all Christian conduct and relationships. It is how we stand before Christ that really matters, and how conduct reflects or damages that relation which really counts. It is through faith and trust alone that anyone can stand before God. As Israel (2:17–29) and Gentiles (11:17–24) had to be warned against presumption before God, so Christians too need to recall their primary responsibility before the Lord (vv. 8, 12) and that all will stand together, weak and strong, before the judgment seat of God (v. 10). It is God's judgment which alone counts.

PRAYER

Lord, help us to recognize how restricted is our own view of you and of your will for humankind. Open us to the reality that some (or many) we cannot tolerate are already accepted by you. Grant us the sense of dependence on you which enables us to practise our different views in thankfulness.

The APPEAL *to the* STRONG

Christian liberty

The second part of Paul's appeal is directed to the strong, those who believed themselves free in regard to the ancient Jewish traditions of clean and unclean and sabbath. Not only were they probably in the majority in the Roman congregations, but Paul also clearly counted himself among the strong. More to the point, Paul evidently believed that the greater responsibility lay with the strong. Those who recognize the full scope of Christian liberty on matters of disputed conduct have the greater responsibility in the exercise of that liberty towards those who feel themselves more constrained.

Paul's first main point is the same as with the weak. The liberty of the strong is and can only be based on *faith*. With them, too, the relation of trust in God through Christ is what determines acceptable conduct for each. Paul states his own position clearly, unequivocally siding with the strong: 'I know and am convinced in the Lord Jesus that nothing is unclean in itself' (v. 14). The reference to 'the Lord Jesus' is in fact twofold. For one thing, the language Paul uses echoes Jesus' own teaching on clean and unclean, particularly in the form in which it was recorded by Mark (Mark 7:15). In other words, Paul was taking care to root the authority for his views in the remembered teaching of Jesus. His decision to abandon the laws of clean and unclean was not a matter of personal pique. It was a decision reached by one who sought to model his lifestyle on that of Jesus himself.

But Paul also came to his conclusion 'in the Lord Jesus' (v. 14). His decision was no arbitrary or simplistic reading of what Jesus had said. He had reflected before God (14:5–6) as to what should be his attitude in a matter of continuing disagreement. His concern was to serve Christ and to please God (v. 18). He wanted his conduct and relationships to grow out of faith (14:23). When that is truly the motivation, then there can be real hope that agreement can be reached regarding disputes.

Proper priorities

If the weak have a responsibility to accept the strong as fellow Christians, the strong also have a responsibility to recognize the scruples of the weak and to respect them as true brothers and sisters in the Lord. The antidote to both diseases of the Christian community is genuine acceptance of and respect for the integrity of the other. This includes the more liberal welcoming the more conservative, not only as an opportunity to instruct and 'enlighten' their scruples (14:1). Although Paul took the opportunity afforded by his letter to give what instruction he thought appropriate, he also recognized that there were many instances where it was better and more beneficial for community if people kept their opinions to themselves (14:22).

It was all a question of priorities. 'The kingdom of God is not a matter of eating and drinking, but of righteousness, peace and joy in the Holy Spirit' (v. 17). Note again the echo of Jesus' own teaching and example. The kingdom of God had been the chief theme of Jesus' preaching (e.g. Mark 1:15). He identified the Spirit's power (in exorcism) with the kingdom's presence in his ministry (Matthew 12:28). He lived out the kingdom's presence in his table-fellowship with tax-collectors and sinners (Matthew 11:19). Paul seems to be echoing all this and drawing on these memories of what Jesus said and did to formulate the resultant priorities for social involvement and conduct. Christ indicates the only priorities that finally count.

But that cut both ways. It certainly meant that belonging to the kingdom of God did not depend on such matters of conduct or of abstaining, as the logic of the more conservative implied. But in that case, neither should the more liberal make a fuss about such more conservative scruples. As Paul had probably already found for himself, liberals could be as fundamentalist in their insistence on the rightness of their position as any conservative. Once again, the antidote in both cases is to keep clear on the primacy of the relationship of faith and to make the benefit of the other a much higher priority than one's own views and advancement (14:19). Love God and your neighbour as yourself.

PRAYER

Lord, Christian liberty is such a precious but also such a fragile flower. Help us properly to cherish it. Make us constantly aware when we threaten it, whether by our tendencies to restrict it to our own preferences or by our selfish abuse of it in disregard for others.

ONCE AGAIN: LOVE IS *the* ANSWER

The principle of the weaker brother

Christian liberty must always be practised in love, otherwise it will certainly be abused. Paul himself is one of the best exemplars of this principle. Although he was himself one of the strong (14:14), his concern throughout this section is to defend the right of the more conservative to hold their scruples, and to condition the behaviour of the more liberal to make it possible for the more conservative to do so in integrity. The principle to which he appeals, as consistently from 12:9 onwards, is, once again, love—the love of neighbour (13:8–10) expressed in this case towards the Christian brother and sister (14:15). How does this love express itself?

First, once again, it means that the strong must respect the weak's scruples. Paul was keenly aware that the designation of some foods as unclean was still a fearful reality for many of his fellow Christians. It was no good insisting to such folk that nothing was unclean in itself and expecting them thereafter to be able to eat pork or whatever without any qualm of conscience. They couldn't do it. Paul accepts that; he respects their scruples and does not dismiss them: 'to the one who reckons something profane, to that person it is profane' (14:14). Here speaks the true Christian liberal, in affirming so strongly a view he personally refuted.

Second, the strong must be prepared to restrict their own liberty for the sake of the weak. Paul envisages situations where the actions of the strong may cause offence to, or bring about the downfall of, the weak (14:13, 15). In such circumstances Paul is clear: even if eating meat or drinking wine is fine in itself, it is quite wrong to do so if to do so causes one's fellow Christian to stumble (vv. 20–21).

This counsel is often designated 'the principle of the weaker brother'. More conservative Christians can sometimes use it almost to require the more liberal to restrict their liberty, rather than as a principle applied by the more liberal themselves to their own conduct. Note, then, that when Paul talks of 'offence' or 'stumbling' he has in mind something much more serious than feelings of outrage or disappointment. He has in view the sort of situation envisaged in the parallel passage in 1 Corinthians 8:10 where the weaker brother is emboldened by the action of the strong to eat forbidden food against his conscience. Such conduct Paul regards as serious sin, as acting contrary to one's faith (vv. 22–23). In so doing, one may be destroying one's faith and one's relation with Christ (14:15, 20). That's how serious the situation has to be before Paul calls on the principle of the weaker brother. In other, apparently similar situations, he was clear that such a principle did not apply, and that what was at stake in the pressure exerted by the more traditionalist believers was the truth of the gospel itself (Galatians 2:11–21).

The impression made on others

Paul was also conscious that the Christian house groups would all the while be making impressions on neighbours and colleagues. The way Christians treated one another would be observed and noted. There would be opportunities for outsiders and unbelievers to be brought in as guests to various gatherings or even to slip through the open street door (1 Corinthians 14:23–25). Paul was therefore anxious that the differences of opinion would not lead to disregard for one another or to a factional spirit within the house churches. 'Do not let your good be brought into contempt' (14:16). The service of Christ should express itself in a concern for one another which would be impressive among the neighbours (14:18).

Such quiet, non-verbal apologetic and evangelism should never be ignored and will often be the most effective witness that small congregations can engage in. What is particularly worthy of note in this instance is the link between internal relationships within a congregation and its wider relationships with those outside the congregation. Internal feuds cannot help but weaken a church's witness. A congregation cannot be built up either if it neglects the impression it makes on those who live about it, or if it allows some of its members to be treated with contempt.

PRAYER

*Fill us, O Lord, with such love for one another that we delight
to give precedence to the needs of others and do not count it
a shame or failure when our wishes for ourselves are given a
lower priority. Help us to pursue what makes for peace
and for the building up of one another.*

78 ROMANS 15:1–6

CHRIST SHOWS *the* WAY

Let each please his neighbour

Paul climaxes his teaching on what Christians should do when they disagree, by referring once again to Christ. It surprises many that Paul does not refer much more often and more explicitly to the teachings of Jesus, as subsequently collected in the Gospels. They usually deduce from this the conclusion that Paul knew little and cared less about the teaching and ministry of Jesus (beyond his cross and resurrection). That is almost certainly the wrong deduction. It is much more likely that in establishing churches the founding apostles took care to familiarize new converts with the key emphases of Jesus' life and teaching, much as the later Gospel writers did by means of their Gospels. In turn, Paul could assume the churches' familiarity with that Gospel tradition in its oral form, and could refer to it when desired. In so doing, he did not need to cite Jesus as the actual speaker being quoted or to quote his very words. Rather he could assume that such allusions as he made to the Jesus tradition would probably be recognized, if only by the church's teachers, for later filling out and elaboration if necessary. Jesus' teaching and the memory of his life, in other words, were not preserved as a formal exercise. Rather the memory of them entered into the life-blood of the churches and helped shape their life and character.

All this is evident in the section of the letter under examination. We have already noted the clear echoes of Jesus' teaching in 12:14 (Matthew 5:44; Luke 6:27–28) and 13:8–10 (Mark 12:28–31) in particular. Within the present treatment of disagreements about clean and unclean food, we have noted the echo of Mark 7:15 in 14:14, as also the echo of Jesus' teaching on the kingdom and his practice of exorcism and table-fellowship (see Study 76). But lest there be any doubt, it becomes explicitly clear in 15:1–3 that Paul had the pattern of Jesus' own teaching and conduct very much in mind in all this. His encouragement to 'please the neighbour' (v. 2) is the only other use in Paul, outside of Romans 13:9–10 and Galatians 5:14, of the word 'neighbour'. It can hardly be doubted that in all three cases Paul had in mind the memory of Jesus' own teaching on the vital necessity to 'love your neighbour as yourself'. And Paul goes on immediately to cite Jesus as the pattern for those who seek to please not themselves but their neighbour (v. 3). That will include reference to Jesus' death, no doubt; but it surely includes also an allusion to Jesus' own personal relationships during his ministry.

Once again, then, Paul puts the onus of responsibility on those who are 'the strong' (in faith), whose strength is to be expressed not so much in liberty of conduct as in concern to 'please' others. Liberty is expressed more in the self-restriction of liberty as in its expression.

The instruction of scripture

As before also (particularly 12:14–21), Paul draws on the accumulated wisdom of scripture—not simply because it would please the weak, but because he himself looked so regularly to scripture for instruction, patience, comfort and hope (v. 4). The reason why he chose the text in this case—'the reproaches of those who reproach you have fallen on me' (Psalm 69:9)—is not immediately obvious. Psalm 69 itself is one of the most powerful cries of personal distress in the Psalter. It was, then, one of those texts which became luminous with meaning in the light of Jesus' suffering and death, and is one of the most quoted in the New Testament (cf. Mark 15:23, 36; John 2:17; 15:25; 19:28–29; Acts 1:20). Its citation here is more apposite than is at first apparent. In the psalm, one devoted to the Lord laments his affliction at the hands not only of his enemies, but also, it seems, of his own people and kinsfolk (Psalm 69:8, 28). Implied, then, is the sort of sharp differences over what loyalty to God and covenant requires, which Paul knew only too well. Jesus, like the psalmist, had experienced much misunderstanding and criticism. His first followers should expect no better. And when such proves to be the case, Jesus' own response should provide precedent and inspiration.

The closing prayer (vv. 5–6) sums up the essentials for community living—harmony as the immediate objective, Jesus Christ as the pattern, and the united glorification of God as the final goal.

PRAYER

Praise be to you, O God, that in Jesus Christ you have provided not only a Saviour but also a pattern for principle, priority and practice in relationships. Grant us always to seek to live 'in accordance with Jesus Christ'.

79   ROMANS 15:7–13

JEW FIRST *but* ALSO GENTILE

God's truth

This paragraph sums up not simply the preceding exhortation, but also the primary thrust of Paul's whole gospel as expounded in the letter. It certainly sums up 14:1—15:6: 'Welcome one another' (v. 7). At the heart of the breakdown in relationships between fellow Christians in Rome was the failure truly to respect the differences of the other, truly to accept others as fellow Christians. And where the onus lay initially with the 'strong' (14:1), Paul now sums up the responsibility even-handedly: 'Welcome one another'. Without such mutual acceptance, without such mutual respect, there could be no harmony or community.

The pattern or precedent is once again Christ: 'as Christ also welcomed you' (v. 7; the echo is of 14:3–4 in particular). Those who found it hard genuinely to respect and accept others should always recall that everything started from Christ's acceptance of each one, themselves included. If Christ could accept me, how can I fail to accept others?

On the broader front, to take the example of Christ seriously meant that Gentile converts needed to recognize the priority of Israel within God's purposes. Christ became 'servant of the circumcised' (v. 8)—born as a Jew, his message and ministry first and foremost for Jews (perhaps echoing Mark 10:43–45). 'God's truth' here comes from the same vocabulary as God's righteousness and faithfulness (cf. 3:3–7). Paul remained convinced of the consistency of God's purpose in first choosing Israel to be his special people, so confirmation of 'the promises of the fathers' (9:4, 7–12; 11:16–18, 28–29) was a high priority in Jesus' ministry and remains a fundamental element in Christian thought and self-understanding. Gentile believers should never forget that. The 'truth of the gospel' is first and foremost the role of Israel.

But also the Gentiles

But that could never be the whole of the gospel for Paul, apostle to the Gentiles. On the contrary, it was precisely his mission within

174

earliest Christianity and earliest Christian theology to state and fight for the rights of Gentiles within this essentially Jewish heritage. So many of his statements on the theme come across now as unbalanced and overstated—inevitable in the crises and accusations he so often had to face. But here he achieves one of his most balanced statements, by citing scripture.

Precisely how Paul intended the beginning of verse 9 to follow from verse 8 is not clear. Perhaps the awkwardness of the grammar reflects the awkwardness Paul still found in his attempt to link the gospel's openness to Gentiles with God's original purpose with and through Israel. At any rate, he was able to cite a little collection of texts which expressed the balance he was attempting to achieve. Quite possibly he had held these texts back (they would have served very well in chapters 9—11) to provide just the rounding off he wanted. Verse 9 quotes Psalm 18:49 (which is identical to 2 Samuel 22:50); verse 10 quotes Deuteronomy 32:43; verse 11 quotes Psalm 117:1; and verse 12 quotes Isaiah 11:10.

The point is that this sequence of texts envisaged what Paul himself now saw as beginning to happen, and not least through his own ministry. Gentiles were singing praises to God with his people; all the nations were beginning to praise the Lord; Gentiles as well as Israel were coming to put their hope in the root of Jesse. If Gentile believers needed to recall Jewish priority and the Jewish character of the gospel, then Jewish believers needed to remember what was God's ultimate purpose. Gentiles should never forget that they were called through Jews, and Jews that their own calling had Gentiles in view from the first. Clearly implied is Paul's conviction that God's glory can only be complete when there is such united and universal praise.

The language of the final prayer (v. 13) is rich and immoderate, reminding the audiences of their dependence on God through his Holy Spirit for all faith and hope, and relishing the experience of joy and peace.

PRAYER

We praise you that 'Jew and Gentile' means 'everyone'.
Prevent us from splitting the one back into two by our suspicions
and jealousies. Help us truly to accept one another, in order that
our praise may be with one voice and one spirit.

PAUL ASSESSES HIS CAREER *to* DATE

Having completed the main thrust of his exposition of the gospel which he had been given as an apostle, Paul begins to draw his lengthy letter to a close. His letter closures usually included some information on his travel plans and requests for prayer, as well as his own prayer for peace, additional greetings and a concluding grace. In this case, however, it soon becomes clear that his travel plans have more weighty objectives in view than simply visiting the Roman churches themselves. It becomes clear, indeed, that Paul's missionary work has reached a critical juncture, and that its whole future will depend on what happens over the next few months and on the way the Roman churches themselves respond to the letter. Hence he approaches the matter of his travel plans by briefly passing in review his career thus far as missionary to the Gentiles.

The priestly work of the gospel

He begins with a typically gracious compliment, in which he expresses his confidence in the Romans' maturity and ability to handle the sort of tensions and difficulties in relationships just addressed (v. 14). Whether Paul was quite as confident as he appears may be doubted in view of the exhortation in chapter 14; but any teacher knows that a blend of compliment and encouragement with instruction and rebuke is likely to be the most effective teaching method.

Paul rounds off his lengthy letter by 'reminding' them of his commission from God (v. 15; cf. 1:5-6). He knew well that his apostleship was a matter of some controversy in some circles (cf. Galatians 1:1, 11-12). So if he was to hope for the support of the churches in Rome, which he himself had had no hand in founding (contrast 1 Corinthians 9:1-2), he had to demonstrate his apostleship, the terms both of his gospel (Romans 1—11) and of his commission.

Paul saw his commission in priestly terms (v. 16)—to be 'a minister (more specifically 'an officiating priest') of Christ Jesus'; 'serving the gospel of God as a priest', where the term denotes the priestly offering of sacrifice; 'in order that the offering of the Gentiles might be acceptable, set apart by the Holy Spirit'. It was not that he saw himself belonging to an order of priesthood distinct from other believers: he had already used priestly language in describing Christians' daily responsibility (12:1). The point is rather that the old distinction between priest and non-priest (lay) no longer applied for Paul. More to the point, the old distinction between clean (Israel) and unclean (Gentiles) had been broken through: it is now the Gentiles themselves (Gentile converts) who are the offering acceptable to God, by virtue not of ritual purification but of being set apart by the Holy Spirit.

Paul's grand strategy

It was with this commission that Paul had exercised his apostolic mission. The strategy was clear. 'From Jerusalem and in a sweep round to Illyricum' (v. 19) actually covered the north-east quadrant of the Mediterranean, round to the very border with Italy, the Roman homeland itself. This would include in particular the Aegean area, which the account in Acts confirms was the main centre of Paul's work as a missionary independent of Antioch (Acts 15:36—20:38). There is no reason to doubt Paul's own testimony as to the success of that mission—'by word and deed, by the power of signs and wonders, by the power of God's Spirit' (vv. 18–19), though elsewhere he shows less confidence in the evidence of 'signs and wonders' (2 Corinthians 12:1–13).

Paul clearly felt that his work in this territory was now finished: 'I have completed the gospel of Christ' (v. 19). By that he hardly meant that he had preached and established churches in every city and town. He must rather mean that he had established firm roots for the gospel in the main cities where he had worked, and from which missionaries went forth through the surrounding region. He could now leave the work of consolidation and further evangelism to the Christian churches themselves—an interesting strategy and one worth pondering.

PRAYER

We praise you, O God, for the ministry and success of your servant, the apostle Paul, through whom we who are Gentiles owe our own faith and calling. Grant us a vision like his, the conviction and commitment to pursue it, and the grace which confirms and prospers it.

PAUL'S VISION *for* HIS FUTURE WORK

Rome as base for mission to Spain

Paul did not simply want to visit the Roman churches. Pleasurable as that would be (15:24, 32; cf. 1:11–12), it was not the primary purpose for the visit.

The principal reason was to solicit Rome's support for the next major stage in Paul's missionary outreach. Having 'completed' the Aegean phase of his mission, he believed he no longer had scope in these regions (v. 23), and was ready to move to the next phase, the north-west quadrant of the Mediterranean, to Spain (v. 24), and possibly beyond to Gaul. The language used ('to be sent on my way') is itself a request for assistance, by providing food, money and letters of introduction, arranging transport, commissioning companions and fellow workers, and so on. By stressing, as usual, his longing to see them, and adding his usual apology for the delays which had prevented an earlier visit (v. 22), together with his disclaimer about building on another's foundations (15:20) and the inference that they were regarded as supporters in wider mission than simply those to be ministered to, Paul evidently hoped to strike the right balance in his relations with these hitherto unvisited churches.

Why Spain?

The reasoning behind Paul's strong desire to press beyond Rome is not clear. Surely helping the gospel to root itself securely in the capital city was goal enough? But the principle of 15:20 was an important one for Paul, and Spain was the next obvious landfall for a Mediterranean traveller. The Phoenicians had long ago brought the east end of the Mediterranean into contact with the west end, having founded Gades (Cadiz) many centuries before. And following the defeat of Carthage at the end of the third century BC, the Romans had been steadily expanding their influence over the Spanish peninsula. Whether there were already many Jews settled in Spain, we do not know. But Paul's usual practice of starting a fresh mission from a synagogue base may well suggest that he knew of at least some Jewish colonies.

More to the point, Spain would be the next natural objective for someone who thought of Jerusalem to Illyricum as a single sweep or arc of a circle (15:19). Perhaps Paul saw his apostolic commission as extending along the northern side of the Mediterranean, with others, in that case, presumably responsible for the southern side (thus completing the circle?). Spain, with the vastness of the Atlantic Ocean behind it, may well have been regarded as 'the ends of the earth'—a fitting end point for an apostle with a universal gospel.

Perhaps still more to the point, we should probably attempt to correlate Paul's missionary goals with what he had said in 11:13–15, with the significance he saw in the conversion of so many Gentiles (15:16) and with the importance of his other main concern at this point, the collection for Jerusalem (bearing verse 27 in mind). Paul evidently saw his work as playing a vital role in the final events of history: by his success in evangelizing Gentiles, he hoped to spur Israel into belated acceptance of the gospel, and thus to set in train the events climaxing in the final resurrection (11:13–15). Israel's scriptures had long looked for those final days when Gentiles would come in as proselytes, bringing their own gifts in homage to Israel's God. Could it be, then, that Paul saw Spain as the place from which the final body of Gentile converts would come, to make up that final pilgrimage, bringing with them converted Israel as that final offering to the Lord, as Isaiah 66:19–20 had predicted?

All this becomes more than a little speculative. And to tie Paul's vision down to such specifics might well make it all the more remote and strange to readers of the 21st century. But if it was a vision as large as that which inspired Paul, we need to know it, whatever the difficulties it may create for our translation of such a vision across the centuries. Certainly the lesser visions of later generations have rarely compared with Paul's either in scope or in the success with which they were translated into effect.

PRAYER

Lord, the Paul whose memory we admire and revere is also strange to us in his vision and hopes. Help us to understand his vision and motivation better. But still more grant us a vision and drive which will stir and stimulate us as his did Paul.

The COLLECTION for JERUSALEM

A sign of solidarity and gratitude

The other primary concern at this point in Paul's letter was about his great ambition to take a collection from his Gentile-founded churches to help relieve the poverty of many of the Christians in Jerusalem. We do not know why the need for financial support had arisen in the Jerusalem church. Had the early community been somewhat rash—selling off capital goods (in expectation of Christ's imminent return)? But other factors could well have been the lack of a strong financial base in Jerusalem for the Galileans, the rapid growth of faith in Jesus Messiah among lower-income groups, and some local famine conditions (cf. Acts 11:29).

Be that as it may, the need to maintain some sort of welfare service for the poor was early recognized (Galatians 2:10) and, of course, accorded with Israel's strong traditions of welfare relief for the poor, the widow, the orphan and the stranger (e.g. Deuteronomy 24:10–22). Paul had accorded similar concerns the same level of importance in his list of charisms in Romans 12:8. He had also engaged himself and his churches to provide such relief from an early stage in his missionary work. It was for this reason (and apparently no other) that Paul made his last journey to Jerusalem (15:25).

Why this should be so is clear enough from what he says here.

• Pre-eminently it was a sign of the Gentile churches' gratitude to Jerusalem for the spiritual blessings they had received from Israel (15:27). In so saying, Paul reaffirms the Jewish roots and character of the gospel and of the blessings it had brought to believing Gentiles (cf. 9:3–4; 11:16–18).

• It was also an expression of how Paul saw the body of Christ working—not just at local, individual church level, but in the inter-relationships of the various churches themselves. Paul uses both the words 'grace' and 'fellowship' (15:26; 2 Corinthians 8:4–7) to describe the collection.

• In particular, this act of Christian generosity across the ocean, Paul no doubt hoped, is what would hold the Gentile churches in union with the mother church in Jerusalem. For all that Paul insisted on his independent commission as apostle to the Gentiles, he had no desire to establish a Gentile Christianity which was cut off from the commitment to Messiah Jesus within Jerusalem and the land of Israel.

A risky endeavour

At the same time, however, Paul had no illusions as to the risks of his plans. He appeals to the Roman Christians 'to contend along with me in your prayers to God on my behalf' (v. 30). His evident concern was twofold. On the one hand, he actually feared for his life at the hands of Jews in Judea. This fits quite well with the picture in Acts of many traditional Jews being violently opposed to Paul and some quite ready to act violently against him (Acts 21:27–36; 23:12–22). More serious, so far as Paul was concerned, he was actually afraid that his 'service for Jerusalem might (not) be acceptable to the saints (in Jerusalem)', that is, that the church in Jerusalem might reject his gift from the Gentile churches. This too fits well with the scenario sketched in Acts, where James, the leader of the Jerusalem church, pointed out to Paul that thousands had been converted, that 'they were all zealous for the law', and that they had been told that Paul was effectively an apostate from the law (Acts 21:20–21).

Indeed, the silence of Acts itself on the subject of the collection is ominous. It may well be that the collection was indeed rejected, as Paul had feared—perhaps because to accept the collection would have been to accept these churches which were functioning on terms which no Jew 'zealous for the law' could recognize. In their view, this collection, however generous, could not begin to serve as that tribute of Gentile proselytes, the wealth of the nations flowing into Jerusalem, for which the prophets had looked (e.g. Isaiah 45:14; 60:5–17). If this was the case, the outcome of Paul's great ambition to re-establish and to seal Christian unity was no more successful than the ecumenical attempts of more recent centuries. The fact should give us no cause of consolation over our own failures on this front.

PRAYER

Lord, we recall that great tradition of care for the poor
and disadvantaged which is consistent throughout the scriptures.
Forgive us our failures of Christian love and renew us in our
practical commitment to the poor.

The HOUSE CHURCHES *of* ROME

How could Paul know so many people in a church he had neither founded nor previously visited? The answer is simple. As the capital city of the empire, 'all roads led to Rome'. There were many business people (like Aquila and Priscilla), or clients or messengers, who would be moving back and forward to Rome (Aquila and Priscilla had connections with three great cities—Rome, Corinth and Ephesus). And Paul's personal links to several of those greeted are notable (vv. 3–4, 5, 8, 9, 13).

Earliest Roman Christianity

It is a curious fact that Paul never speaks of 'the church in Rome' (contrast 1 Corinthians 1:2; 1 Thessalonians 1:1). The only 'church' in Rome which he mentions is the church that met in the house of Aquila and Priscilla (v. 5). This could be accidental, but it could also reflect two facts of relevance. One is that the extensive Jewish community in Rome had a good many synagogues (we know of about ten or more), but it did not have a central organization or governing body, as was the case, for example, in Alexandria. Perhaps the Christian community, still in the shadow of the Jewish, was similarly lacking in a central organization. The other fact is that, almost certainly, the number of Christian believers or adherents far exceeded the capacity of any single house to contain it, whereas 'the whole church' in Corinth could evidently meet in the house of Gaius (v. 23). And Paul's use of the term 'church' suggests that in using it he had in mind primarily the Christian believers gathered together 'in church', to be church (1 Corinthians 11:18). In other words, there was no central building, a church, for the first Christians in Rome. As elsewhere, the only 'churches' (meeting places), by and large, were the private homes of individuals.

When we study Romans 16 closely, it is possible to discern several household groupings: the church in the house of Aquila and Priscilla (v. 5); possibly also churches consisting of believers belonging to the families of Aristobulus and of Narcissus (vv. 10–11); possibly also the final groupings mentioned in verse 14 (Asyncritus, Phlegon, Hermes, Patrobas, Hermas, and the brothers with them), and verse

15 (Philologus, Julia, Nereus and his sister, and Olympas, and all the saints with them). So it would be more accurate to speak of 'the *churches* of Rome' at the beginning of Rome's Christian history than of 'the *church* of Rome'.

House church Christianity

If we take seriously the fact of house churches as the only churches, it raises further issues. For one thing, the quality and size of most houses would mean that only those well-to-do would be able to host the church gatherings. There would be a dependency of local churches on those members with higher incomes and suitably sized property. The fact also that most of the names listed in Romans 16 were common among slaves and freedmen/women suggests that such well-to-do members were few (cf. 1 Corinthians 1:26). And the likelihood is that patronage and leadership would go together. In other words, the churches from the beginning would be subject to all-too-familiar social and economic pressures.

For another, the size of even well-to-do houses would not permit more than about 30 to 45 to meet at any one time. Even if Gaius had a particularly splendid house, the likelihood of 'the whole church' in Corinth exceeding about 60 is small (v. 23). For those today who lament the passing of large congregations of hundreds or even thousands, it is salutary to remember that at the period of the Church's most vigorous growth, the individual congregations were of a size which most denominations would today reckon as failure.

Another thought worth considering is the fact that houses were doubling as both churches and households. This could explain part of the tensions caused by women's ministry. For as wife within a *household*, the woman was bound to defer to the male head of the household. But as a prophet within the *church*, she might be called to exhort or instruct others, including her husband. Some such circumstances seem to be behind the tensions between 1 Corinthians 11:2–16 and 14:34–36.

PRAYER

Lord, we bless your name for these early gatherings in your name and for the impact they made on surrounding neighbours and friends. Rekindle in the churches of today that character and effectiveness of witness.

The MINISTRY of WOMEN

One of the most striking features of Romans 16 is the prominent roles of responsibility and ministry attributed in it to various women.

Phoebe

Phoebe (v. 1) evidently had business in Rome (the language used may indicate a lawsuit), and may have been the bearer of the letter itself. Whatever the facts, Paul took the opportunity provided by the letter to introduce her to the churches in Rome.

She was a 'deacon of the church of Cenchreae' (one of Corinth's port cities). Note that Paul says 'deacon', not 'deaconess'. That ministry role could cover or include different kinds of ministry (cf. 12:7; 13:4; 15:8; 1 Corinthians 16:15). Whatever the responsibility was, it had cohered into a title—'deacon' (cf. Philippians 1:1). Together with apostle, prophet and teacher, 'deacon' was one of the first 'official' ministries to emerge in this way. And the first to be so designated in the history of Christianity was a woman, Phoebe.

Phoebe is also described by Paul as *prostatis* (v. 2). Modern translators have usually given it little weight; hence RSV's translation 'helper'. But in fact the term denoted a patron, or benefactor. Phoebe was evidently a wealthy woman, able to provide weighty financial and/or social support for the church in Cenchreae. She was probably, therefore, one of the leading figures in that church.

Priscilla

No woman appears so often in Paul's company as Priscilla. She was the wife of Aquila, tentmakers by profession, with branches of their business, it would seem, in several large cities (Acts 18:18–19; 1 Corinthians 16:19). They were evidently prosperous, able to travel extensively (probably with slaves or associates to whom they could entrust the care of their different branches), hospitable (Acts 18:2–3, 26), and committed to the extent of risking their own necks in the support they gave to Paul (v. 4).

Judging by the fact that she is named before her husband in several references, Priscilla was the more dominant of the two. This leading role probably came to expression in their Christian affairs, including the instruction given to Apollos in Acts 18:26, and the leadership of the churches which they invited to meet in their house (here and 1 Corinthians 16:19). The high regard in which they were both held by 'all the churches of the Gentiles' (v. 5) suggests a much wider sponsorship and support for many small groups of Christians round the north-east Mediterranean than we have record of, and Priscilla would no doubt have been to the forefront in that minstry.

Junia

In recent centuries, the name here (v. 7) has usually been translated as Junias (male), on the assumption that no woman could be so described! But 'Junias' was not at all known as a name at the time, whereas 'Junia' was a common female name. Almost certainly, then, Andronicus and Junia were man and woman, probably husband and wife. The point is that Andronicus and Junia are described here as 'outstanding among the apostles, who were in Christ before me' (v. 7), the reference being, presumably, to the wider circle of apostles mentioned by Paul in 1 Corinthians 15:7. Since Paul usually thought of apostles as church founders (cf. 1 Corinthians 9:1–2), and since Andronicus and Junia are the only apostles mentioned by Paul in connection with the churches of Rome, the intriguing possibility emerges that one of the apostolic founders of the church in Rome was a woman!

Mary, Tryphaena, Tryphosa and Persis

Among the other women mentioned by Paul in Romans 16 are these four, praised particularly for their 'hard working' (vv. 6, 12). This is a term which Paul uses elsewhere in commending those whose leadership ought to be recognized (cf. 1 Corinthians 16:16; 1 Thessalonians 5:12). And in Romans 16, they are the only people so described. We may conclude, therefore, that the churches of Rome were particularly blessed by the quality and quantity of women's ministry and leadership.

PRAYER

We praise you for the too-often unsung ministry of women within the churches of Christ. Forgive us that it has for so long been overlooked or trivialized. And enable us to recognize and benefit more fully from the rich diversity of ministry which you give to your people.

A FINAL PERSONAL NOTE

Do not relax your guard

Quite why Paul interjected this paragraph is not at all clear. The sudden warning is surprising, though not dissimilar to Philippians 3:2–21 and Galatians 6:11–15. Certainly it was his style to take the pen from his scribe and to add a few final words in his own hand (cf. Galatians 6:11–18). But why such a sombre note on this occasion? The most likely answer is a combination of Paul's personal experience and a final recollection of the situation of the Roman churches. Paul had experienced all too often 'those who cause divisions and temptations contrary to the teaching' which his readers had received (v. 17). And the threats to Christian existence in the capital city, already reflected in 12:14—13:7, might have welled up once again in Paul's prayerful concern for them.

It is evident, however, that Paul did not have anyone particular in mind. The language used is not specific but refers vaguely to 'those who cause divisions and temptations' (v. 17). The attack on gluttony, 'those who serve only their belly' (v. 18), is well established Jewish polemic against what was perceived as apostasy. 'Smooth (plausible) speech' and 'fine-sounding words' likely to 'deceive the hearts of the unsuspecting' (v. 18) echoes characteristic warnings in Jewish wisdom literature lest the piety of the simple be subverted by malicious scoffers. In other words, this is the warning of one who himself relished the subtlety and profundity of the gospel, but who was all too conscious that there were others well able to distort such subtleties. The summons, then, is a general one, to be on their guard against tendencies to factionalism, always to weigh motives of personal gain, and to be circumspect in regard to all plausible-sounding arguments which led away from the central truths of the gospel.

The call, it should be noted, is not to avoid disagreements as such, nor for simplicity for simplicity's sake. The concern was rather for the right interaction of wisdom and simplicity—'wise in regard to what is good, and innocent in regard to what is evil' (v. 19)—a combination which requires all the maturity of shared experience evaluated in the light of the gospel's priorities of commitment to God through

Christ and of love of neighbour as of first and foremost importance.

The hope of Satan being 'crushed under foot' (v. 20) sums up the traditional Jewish and Christian hope for the final defeat of every power hostile to God. An allusion to Genesis 3:15 is probable: Paul always sees the end in the light of the beginning, and the beginning in the light of the end. The usual Pauline final grace ('the grace of our Lord Jesus be with you') likewise sums up Christian confidence in terms of the word ('grace', divine generosity) which more than any other for Paul characterizes the one in whom trust is placed.

Other friends of Paul

The last brief inclusion of some final greetings is a further reminder of the many associates of Paul. Timothy (v. 21), described as one of his 'fellow workers', was Paul's most frequently mentioned associate in Paul's letters and in Acts. He contributed to no less than six of Paul's letters and was Paul's most trusted lieutenant. Lucius, Jason and Sosipater, Paul describes as 'my kinsmen', a reminder that though so few Jews had accepted the gospel, Paul was by no means the only Jew who had done so and who supported a mission to the Gentiles— as also Andronicus, Junia and Herodion (vv. 7, 11). Tertius (v. 22) acted in this instance as Paul's secretary. Perhaps the freedom Paul gave to his secretaries in dictating his letters explains some of the differences in style between them.

Gaius (v. 23), we have already noted, must have been a wealthy householder, able to accommodate the whole Corinthian church. The importance of hospitality, particularly on the part of the well-to-do, is again underlined. Erastus was 'the city treasurer', presumably a high financial officer within the local government of Corinth; we may even have an inscription commemorating a benefaction he had bestowed on the city. Quartus, remembered simply as 'the brother', no doubt can be taken as representative of the multitude of early believers whose names are now lost to us.

PRAYER

We are conscious, O God, of how easily the central elements
of the gospel can be subverted and confused. Keep us ever alert
and able to distinguish simple faith from naïvety
and profundity of faith from impressive words.

86 ROMANS 16:25–27

A LATER DOXOLOGY

The way in which Paul intended his letter to end is unclear. Most likely he intended the grace of verse 20 as the end, with verses 21–23 as a kind of postscript, as others clamoured to add their greetings to the letter on its completion. Other scribes later recognized the awkwardness which resulted by transferring the grace of verse 20 to verse 24. It is also evident from the manuscript history that Romans was circulated in an abbreviated version (1:1—14:23), to which a later hand then added this final doxology (vv. 25–27). As the fuller version reasserted itself, the doxology was transferred to this point. And given that the original conclusion seemed to be rather abrupt, it made sense to retain the doxology here. So much we may surmise. The key point is that verses 25–27 were almost certainly not dictated or penned by Paul himself. Nevertheless, they provide a marvellous Pauline summary to Paul's greatest single letter.

The revelation of the mystery

At the heart of the gospel is 'the revelation of the mystery' (v. 25). 'Mystery' was the word which Paul had used to sum up his own solution to the great puzzle of Israel's destiny (11:25). The language used here strengthens the sense of a divine purpose, determined from the first but kept secret 'for long ages'. But it also echoes the more developed use of the term in the later Pauline letters (Colossians 1:26–27; Ephesians 3:3–6). At the heart of the gospel was the unveiling of this mystery, the disclosure of the divine secret. This, of course, is a way of affirming that the astonishing and unexpected turn of events was fully in line with what God had always planned—'in accordance with the command of the eternal God' (v. 26). But it also means that Christianity itself rests on the claim to a fundamentally new insight into God's purposes in creation and revelation.

That new, or rather newly revealed, purpose focused in bringing 'all the nations to the obedience of faith' (v. 26). The scribe who added this doxology repeated, no doubt deliberately, Paul's own phrase in 1:5—Paul's apostolic commission to bring 'to the obedience of faith... all the nations'. It was precisely Paul's special commission to 'make known' this mystery for the benefit of the nations;

again the echo of Colossians 1:25–27 and Ephesians 3:2–6 is strong. In short, this is what Paul perceived as of fresh revelatory significance —that God had always intended to unite Jew and Gentile in one worshipping people, in one faith, as the climax to his saving purpose; and that Paul had been given a special commission to bring that purpose to completion. As the one who added this doxology perceived, we shall never make sense of Paul's theology and contribution to Christianity unless this central thrust of both Paul's theology and mission, for all nations, is rightly appreciated.

To the only wise God

This insight, however, is wholly framed within Paul's monotheistic (inherited Jewish) faith. The doxology is addressed 'to him who is able to strengthen you' (v. 25), reaffirming the rootedness of the whole in God and in his power (cf. 1:16, 20; 4:21; 9:17, 22; 11:23; 14:4). And its final benediction is addressed 'to God only wise' (v. 27). This is one of the classic affirmations of Jewish monotheism (cf. e.g. John 17:3; 1 Timothy 1:17; and earlier Ecclesiasticus 1:8 and 2 Maccabees 1:24–25). Paul affirms the oneness of the only God elsewhere (3:30; 1 Corinthians 8:6). It is important to note how deeply rooted within his native religious heritage Paul was and was perceived still to be, including, not least, at the end of his greatest epistle.

This is all the more true when the qualification is added—'in accordance with my gospel and the preaching of Jesus Christ' (v. 25), 'through Jesus Christ' (v. 27). It is Jesus Christ who is at the heart of the new Christian appreciation of the one God. It is Jesus Christ who brings to light the new revelation of God's hidden purpose. It is through Jesus Christ that Christians draw near to the one God. This 'christological qualification' does not undermine faith in God as one; rather it helps to clarify the universal significance of the one God and to bring that significance to fresh implementation.

PRAYER

The mystery of your ultimate purpose, O God, still has much of mystery about it for us. But we praise you for the insight given into that mystery by your servant Paul. We join with people of all nations in praising you as 'the only wise God, through Jesus Christ'.